The Ghetto fights

GW00468281

This book is published with the aid of the Bookmarks Publishing Cooperative. Many socialists have some savings put aside, probably in a bank or savings bank. While there, this money is being loaned out by the bank to some business or other to further the capitalist search for profit. We believe it is better loaned to a socialist venture to further the struggle for socialism. That's how the cooperative works: in return for a loan, repayable at a month's notice, members receive free copies of books published by Bookmarks. At the time this book was published, the cooperative had 430 members, from as far apart as London and Malaysia, Canada and Norway. Since 1980, the cooperative has helped publish more than fifty books.

Like to know more?

Write to the Bookmarks Publishing Cooperative, 265 Seven Sisters Road, Finsbury Park, London N4 2DE, England.

Bookmarks
London, Chicago and Melbourne

The Ghetto fights

Marek Edelman

with an introduction
by John Rose

The Ghetto fights / *Marek Edelman*
Published by Bookmarks September 1990.
Bookmarks, 265 Seven Sisters Road, London N4 2DE, England
Bookmarks, PO Box 16085, Chicago, IL 60616, USA
Bookmarks, GPO Box 1473N, Melbourne 3001, Australia

First published in Polish in Warsaw, 1945.
English translation first published in New York, May 1946.
Copyright © Marek Edelman; introduction © Bookmarks and John Rose
ISBN 0 906224 56 X

Printed by Cox and Wyman Limited, Reading, England
Cover design by Peter Court

Bookmarks is linked to an international grouping of socialist
organisations:
Australia: *International Socialist Organisation*, GPO Box 1473N,
　　　　Melbourne 3001
Belgium: *Socialisme International,* rue Lovinfosse 60, 4030 Grivegnée
Britain: *Socialist Workers Party*, PO Box 82, London E3
Canada: *International Socialists,* PO Box 339, Station E, Toronto,
　　　　Ontario M6H 4E3
Denmark: *Internationale Socialister*, Ryesgade 8, 3, 8000 Århus C
France: *Socialisme International*, BP 189, 75926 Paris Cedex 19
Germany: *Sozialistische Arbeiter Gruppe,* Wolfgangstrasse 81,
　　　　6000 Frankfurt 1
Greece: *Organosi Sosialistiki Epanastasi*, PO Box 8161, 10010 Omonia,
　　　　Athens.
Holland: *Groep Internationale Socialisten*, PO Box 9720, 3506 GR
　　　　Utrecht.
Ireland: *Socialist Workers Movement,* PO Box 1648, Dublin 8
Norway: *Internasjonale Sosialister,* Postboks 5370, Majorstua, 0304
　　　　Oslo 3
United States: *International Socialist Organization,* PO Box 16085,
　　　　Chicago, IL 60616

Contents

The Warsaw Ghetto

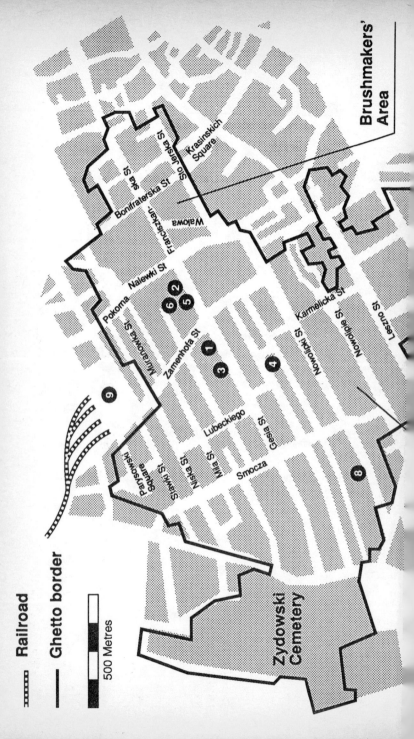

Brushmakers' Area

Krasinskich Square

Bonifraterska St

Sło jelska St

Franciszkan-ska St

Walowa

Nalewki St

Pokorna

Zamenhofa St

Muranowska St

Karmelicka St

Nowolipki St

Nowolipie St

Leszno St

Panysowski Square

Stawki St

Niska St

Mila St

Smocza

Lubeckiego

Gesia St

Zydowski Cemetery

- - - - Railroad

——— Ghetto border

500 Metres

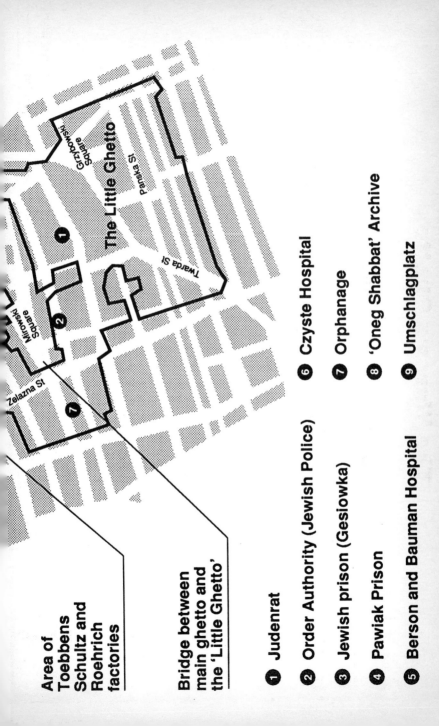

The Little Ghetto

Grzybowski Square

Panska St

Twarda St

Mirowski Square

Zelazna St

Area of
Toebbens
Schultz and
Roehrich
factories

Bridge between
main ghetto and
the 'Little Ghetto'

1 Judenrat

2 Order Authority (Jewish Police)

3 Jewish prison (Gesiowka)

4 Pawiak Prison

5 Berson and Bauman Hospital

6 Czyste Hospital

7 Orphanage

8 'Oneg Shabbat' Archive

9 Umschlagplatz

Authors

Marek Edelman was a member of the Jewish Resistance
Organisation of the Warsaw Ghetto during 1942-43 and a member of
the Jewish Socialist Party of Poland, the Bund. After the war he trained
as a doctor. He now lives in the Polish city of Lodz and is a leading
supporter of the independent trade union Solidarity.

John Rose is the author of **Israel: The hijack state** (Bookmarks
1986) and a member of the Socialist Workers Party in Britain.

Introduction

John Rose

Author's note

The introduction that follows refers to Leon Trotsky. I have never been a supporter of the ideas of Trotsky, which are foreign to me. However if the popularisation of this clearly anti-totalitarian book can become a warning to future generations then it can be published with any introduction.

My agreement to the publication of this edition does not give exclusive rights to Bookmarks for future publications.

Marek Edelman, May 1990.

Introduction

John Rose

1.

IT IS A GREAT HONOUR to introduce **The Ghetto fights**, written by Marek Edelman, to socialists in Britain. This brilliant account of the Jewish struggle against the Nazis in the Warsaw Ghetto during the Second World War was first published in English by the Jewish Socialist Party of Poland, the Bund,[1] in New York at the end of the war. Since then it has all but been forgotten. The Zionist view that the Warsaw Ghetto was a symbol for the Jews on the road to Palestine has tended to dominate the historical treatment of the subject.[2] The alternative view that the Warsaw Ghetto uprising was part of the wider struggle to liberate Poland from the Nazis has been ignored. Yet this was how it was seen by the Jewish Resistance Organisation that led the uprising, of which Marek Edelman was a leading member.

By chance, a copy of **The Ghetto fights** came into the hands of a Jewish journalist, working on **Socialist Worker** in London, who found it in his grannie's attic! It was also re-published in Polish by the Polish government in April 1988 as part of a volume commemorating the 45th anniversary of the Ghetto rising.[3] There is a copy in the British Museum in London and many references to it in all serious accounts of the Warsaw Ghetto. But this is the first time that Edelman's account has been published in full in Britain since the war.

Marek Edelman was one of hundreds of Jewish youngsters who pressed for armed struggle to resist the Nazis from the first days of the building of the Warsaw Ghetto walls. He was the sole survivor of the five-person command group that finally led the uprising. And he was a member of the Bund, which had a fine (and to this day little-known) pre-war record of organising —jointly with the Polish Socialist Party (PPS)—both Jewish and non-Jewish workers' struggles against anti-semitism in Poland.

After the war Edelman stayed in Poland. This was a decision of political principle and remarkable in itself, in the shadow of the Nazi Holocaust and considering his hatred of the Stalinist regime that had imposed itself on Poland. Little was heard of him until he was 're-discovered' by Solidarity journalist Hannah Krall. She found him to be a heart surgeon, continuing the job of trying to save lives that he had begun in the Warsaw Ghetto. She published a series of interviews with him in 1977 in a book titled **Shielding the Flame**. It was an instant best-seller in Poland, selling tens of thousands of copies.[4] It was also turned into a television documentary that has been shown several times on Polish television.

Edelman had been active in the independent trade union Solidarity from the start. During the union's congress in Gdansk in September 1981 one military veteran of the Polish Underground, the wartime resistance movement against the Nazis, stopped the congress celebrations of his own exploits during the war and pointed out that among the delegates was a hero of considerably greater stature: Dr Marek Edelman of the Lodz delegation, the last surviving leader of the Warsaw Ghetto uprising. After the army coup against Solidarity in December 1981, the government of General Jaruzelski tried to bestow 'honours' on Edelman, but he refused to accept them.

In March 1989 I had the good fortune to interview him at his home in the Polish city of Lodz, where he agreed that the Socialist Workers Party could re-publish **The Ghetto fights**.[5]

Why re-publish now? One answer would simply be that this is a unique socialist document of great interest that deserves to be made public. But there is another reason. The 1990s have opened with the collapse of the post-war settlement in Eastern Europe and the Soviet Union. These territories are in turmoil. Great issues of twentieth-century history, buried for

40 years, are bursting into life again. Free-market capitalism is posed as the only alternative to Stalin's 'Communism', which has dominated these countries and is now discredited. Yet it was precisely the crisis of free-market capitalism, in the Great Depression of the 1920s and 1930s, that helped shape the great tragedy of the rise of Hitler, the outbreak of the Second World War and the Nazi Holocaust of the Jews, of which the Warsaw Ghetto is such an important symbol. Stalin's 'Communism' was itself a factor in Hitler's first flush of victory. Any study of the historical background that led to the Warsaw Ghetto would have to include these factors.

Again, the nationalisms of Eastern Europe, oppressed for 40 years, are today coming to the surface, sometimes carrying ancient anti-semitic prejudices in their wake. What is the cause of anti-semitism? Can the history of the struggle of the Warsaw Ghetto, seen as a struggle against anti-semitism, provide some lessons for us as we confront this new development?

In the Middle East another post-war settlement is under fire: the imposition of a Jewish population on Palestine as an attempt to 'solve' Europe's 'Jewish Question' is challenged by the Palestinian Arab *intifada*, an uprising perhaps to be compared with those in Eastern Europe. Zionism has claimed the Warsaw Ghetto as a symbol for itself, stressing the virtue of exclusive Jewish struggle and the failure of non-Jewish solidarity. But a close study of the history of the Ghetto challenges this view. Zionism was ambiguous toward the struggle against the Nazis; it saw the solution for the Jews as lying outside Europe. After 40 years this solution is an abject failure. Perhaps those socialists who demanded unambiguous commitment to Jewish struggle to stay in Europe, and to build solidarity with non-Jewish anti-Nazi forces, offered the best hope 40 years ago and offer the best hope today?

Finally, does the collapse of Stalinism really herald the death of Marxism, as so many of its enemies in the West are trumpeting? Or has there always been an alternative Marxist tradition to the Stalinist version, both in theory and in practice, which a proper treatment of the Warsaw Ghetto might help clarify?

The re-publication of **The Ghetto fights** and the debate among socialists that it will generate will touch on all these great themes. These modest introductory remarks serve merely to point a possible direction for that debate.

Those nervous blips on the screens of the world's stock exchange computers today are a constant reminder that the global capitalist system is quite capable of plunging us into the nightmare of the past that produced Hitler. We need to learn the lessons now. What better starting point for an introduction to the history of the Warsaw Ghetto than one that identifies the crisis of capitalism itself as the ultimate source of barbarity and evil in the twentieth century?

2.

The Wall Street Crash of October 1929 signalled the worldwide economic crisis that threw the capitalist system into the chaos of the 1930s. The Great Slump devastated Germany, throwing six million workers on the dole and ruining thousands of small businessmen, shopkeepers, farmers and self-employed craftsmen. A sense of national inferiority, in any case, had lingered in Germany since the country's defeat in the First World War. The Versailles Treaty, which had compelled Germany to pay massive war reparations, had compounded this mood. The Nazis exploited this. In the elections of 1928 the Nazis had polled only 800,000 votes. In September 1930 they won six and a half million. From being the smallest party in the Reichstag, the German parliament, they became the second largest.

'The heads of Marxists and Jews will soon roll in the sand,' boasted Hitler, as Nazi stormtroopers launched terror campaigns throughout Germany's towns and cities.

However the Communist Party too had increased its share of the votes, from about three million to four and a half million. Although the Social Democrats, the German parliamentary socialists, had lost ground, the two parties together were electorally far more powerful than the Nazis. More important, they represented the vast majority of organised workers who, through their unions and workplaces, were a physical and organisational bulwark against the Nazis.

But the German Communist Party was dominated by Stalin's 'Third Period' policy, which denounced the Social Democrats as 'social fascists', regarding them as the main enemy! Hitler's electoral gains were dismissed as his last big success; the Nazis would soon fade away.

One socialist voice spoke out clearly against this nonsense, that of Leon Trotsky, who by this time had been exiled from Russia by Stalin. Trotsky's writings remain to this day the most original and incisive analysis of both the rise of the Nazis and the worldwide catastrophe created by Stalin and the German Communist Party by their refusal to build a united front with the Social Democrats against the Nazis. This alone could have halted Hitler's rise to power.

Trotsky issued a series of astonishingly prophetic pamphlets and articles that followed each twist and turn of Nazi growth and the failure of the left to respond.[6] Alas, hardly anyone listened. Stalin had commandeered the immense authority that the Russian Revolution of 1917 held over the left. Trotsky was isolated as a 'traitor', his views dismissed as heresies throughout the world Communist movement. Yet had Trotsky's advice been acted upon, Hitler could have been defeated, the Second World War might have been averted, and 50 million people, including six million Jews, need not have been slaughtered.

Trotsky recognised the September 1930 election as a mighty boost for Hitler and an equally mighty setback for the left. He attacked the Communist Party for failing to understand the right-wing radicalisation of the lower middle class, the petty bourgeoisie. The growth of the Nazis was an expression of two factors: the deep social crisis, which had hit the lower middle class particularly hard, and the lack of a revolutionary socialist party to which they could turn for leadership. Such a party, said Trotsky, was 'the party of revolutionary hope'. The Nazis, as a mass movement, fascism, were 'the party of counter-revolutionary despair'.

He wrote after the election:

When revolutionary hope embraces the whole working class, it inevitably pulls behind it considerable sections of the petty bourgeoisie. The election revealed the opposite picture: counter-revolutionary despair embraced the petty-bourgeois mass with such a force that it drew behind it many sections of the working class.[7]

The Nazis expressed the urge of the lower middle class to assert itself against the rest of society. Such people resented their social position: they looked up with envy at big business, whose greater competitiveness frequently forced their own businesses into bankruptcy, and they looked down on the workers, jealous of their ability to organise for their own collective self-defence in trade unions and political parties. As Isaac Deutscher put it:

> Big business, Jewish finance, parliamentary democracy... Marxism, all seemed to merge into a many-headed monster which strangled him. At big business the small man shook his fists, at the worker he shrilled his bourgeois respectability.[8]

It was this anger of the lower middle class, impoverished by the crisis of capitalism, that gave the Nazis their force and impetus. 'Not every small bourgeois going wild can become a Hitler,' said Trotsky, 'but there is something of a Hitler in every small bourgeois going wild.'

Yet at the same time he stressed the essential political weakness of the lower middle class. Amorphous and atomised, it was attracted by the magnet of power. If the organised working class, united and confident, had posed real economic and political solutions to the catastrophe engulfing Germany, Hitler's movement could have been shattered. The manic ferment in the middle of society could have been pulled behind the organised working class, which was the real force for progress.

This analysis of the roots of Nazism as an expression of petty-bourgeois despair also explains its anti-semitism. Abram Leon, the author of the Marxist classic **The Jewish Question** who was himself later killed by the Nazis, wrote:

> The primarily commercial and artisan character of Judaism, heritage of a long historical past, makes it enemy Number One of the petty bourgeoisie on the domestic market. It is therefore the petty-bourgeois character of Judaism which makes it so odious to the petty bourgeoisie.[9]

Hitler borrowed 'The Protocols of Zion', the world Jewish conspiracy theory invented by supporters of the Russian Tsar at the end of the previous century, in order to strengthen and politicise the feelings of anti-semitism of the petty bourgeoisie. It was 'Jewish finance capital' that controlled the German economy and 'Jewish control of the labour movement' that had brought about Germany's ruin, he declared.

As Abram Leon noted, the attack on the Jews allowed the petty bourgeois to be 'anti-capitalist without ceasing to be capitalist'.[10] Additionally, it allowed the Nazis to attack the labour movement while at the same time appealing to German workers to see only Jewish capital, rather than capitalism in general, as their exploiter. Finally, the explicit racism of the Nazis was used to bind all Germany together, especially the workers. Abram Leon wrote:

> The anti-capitalism of the masses, first channelled in the direction of Judaism, is then carried over against the 'foreign enemy', which is identified with Judaism. The 'Germanic race' will find itself faced with the duty of fighting the 'Jew', its principal enemy, in all its disguises: that of domestic Bolshevism [in other words Communism] and liberalism, of Anglo-Saxon plutocracy and of foreign Bolshevism. Hitler states in **Mein Kampf** that it is indispensable to present the various enemies under a common aspect, otherwise there is a danger that the masses will start thinking too much about the differences which exist among those enemies.[11]

Though the roots of fascism are in the despair of the lower middle class, it is nonetheless a form of capitalist rule. Under capitalism the ruling class, which is only a small minority in society, always rules with the support of the petty bourgeoisie. In periods of social stability it leans on the petty-bourgeois leaders, the social-democratic politicians, trade union leaders, social reformers of all kinds. These channels allow negotiation between capitalism and the organised working class; together with minor reforms and concessions, this prevents serious threats to capitalist rule.

But as the capitalist crisis deepens, this situation changes. With increasing unemployment and falling living standards, these channels become less effective in holding back working-class demands. At the same time, there is less profit around to pay for even minor wage increases and social reforms. The deeper the crisis, the more difficult this becomes.

The ruling class then vacillates. This was the situation in Germany in 1930. One section of the ruling class rejected social democracy as no longer effective; another recoiled from the brutality and risk involved in supporting fascism.

In such a situation the left has to respond correctly, otherwise the ruling class will finally allow fascism to replace social democracy, annihilating all workers' organisations. But Trotsky's warnings went unheeded. The cavalier attitude to the Nazis continued. One leading German Communist even made the memorable remark: 'After Hitler, us...' He meant that Hitler would be a push-over. Meanwhile Trotsky was himself denounced as a fascist and counter-revolutionary.

In desperation Trotsky appealed over the heads of the Communist leaders to the rank and file of the party:

> Worker communists! There are hundreds of thousands of you, millions of you... If fascism comes to power it will ride like a terrific tank over your skulls and spines. Your salvation lies in merciless struggle. Only a fighting unity with social-democratic workers can bring victory. Make haste, communist workers, you have very little time to lose.[12]

3.

Stalin crowned his failure to fight Hitler properly before he came to power in 1933 by signing an agreement with him six years later, in August 1939. The Hitler-Stalin Pact was the prelude to the partition of Poland between Nazi Germany and the Soviet Union and the start of the Second World War. Stalin helped Hitler strangle the Polish people. Poland was a weak country, independent for only 20 years, wracked by economic crisis, massive unemployment and anti-semitism. It buckled hopelessly before the Nazi invasion in September 1939.

> Poland formed a huge bulge which fitted into the open jaws of Germany... The jaws bit down, and sabre teeth in the form of armoured columns tore deeply into the flesh of Poland... Poland's forces were all but immobile, armourless and antiquated, her arsenal better suited to war five decades earlier. Sustained by raw courage, Poland asked the horse to fight the tank...
> Death spewed from the skies. Within hours of the German border violations, the Polish air force, tiny and outdated, was shot to pieces on the ground. Within hours, rail lines were ripped up and supply dumps smoked skyward... The Luftwaffe, the Nazi air force, shot down Polish troops running for cover, Polish peasants working in the fields, Polish children in the schoolyards...[13]

The Nazis lost no time in showing the Poles what their occupation would mean. Hitler, who took the victory salute in Warsaw on 5 October 1939, denounced the 'artificial' Polish state, the foster child of Western democracy, which he said was 'to be swept off the face of the earth'. Behind the advancing Nazi front-line troops came the special execution squads.

> Their task was not only to crush resistance and opposition but to slaughter whole categories—the political and intellectual elite, the mentally sick, the leaders of Polish communities—as potential sources of racial and political infection... In annexed regions, the Polish language was forbidden in public, special limited shopping hours were

imposed on Poles, and all education over primary level and cultural activity were forbidden... The food rationing system that was eventually introduced allowed 2613 calories a day to a German, but a mere 669 to a Pole. This was a frankly genocidal policy. Like the Jews, but on a slower time scale, the Poles had been designated as an inferior, vermin-race to be eliminated from physical existence... In the cities there was no safety from the haphazard nature of Nazi terror. At any moment, one might be seized for a labour round-up (and taken for forced labour to Germany or to a concentration camp), arrested as a hostage, or shot in the countless street executions...[14]

Poles fared little better under the Soviet occupation in the east. From February 1940 Stalin began his huge and brutal deportation policy:

Families were driven from their homes and packed into unheated cattle trucks, which headed slowly for Siberia while their occupants stifled, starved or froze to death... Between one and a half and two million Poles were herded into the trains, to be employed as slaves or forced labourers in mines and lumber camps near the Arctic Circle, or to be dumped in the steppes of Kazakhstan... Tens of thousands of Poles who had held official posts were 'tried' and consigned to long sentences in prisons or camps. No reliable figures exist, but it is estimated that anything between a third and a half of the deported Poles were dead by the time of Hitler's attack on the Soviet Union in June 1941.[15]

4.

The policy of herding the Jews into closed ghettos in Poland's towns and cities was the prelude to Hitler's 'Final Solution'. Nearly all of Poland's three million Jews were to perish in the concentration camps—half of the total number of Jews slaughtered in the Nazi Holocaust.

Marek Edelman's **The Ghetto fights** begins with the

Nazi invasion of Poland and the policy of forcing the Jewish communities into the ghettos. It seems almost impertinent to comment on the work itself. It is difficult to improve on the words of the introduction to the Bund's 1945 edition, which said that it achieves 'that which not all masterpieces can achieve... it gives in serious, purposeful, reticent words a record, simple and unostentatious, of a common martyrdom... an authentic document about perseverance and moral strength...'[16]

Yet perhaps the reader needs to be warned just how numbingly depressing is the story of the Ghetto. The Nazis succeeded in deporting two-thirds of the Ghetto population in cattle trucks to the extermination camps without resistance. How can we find the ideas and words to make sense of this? An insight is given in Edelman's remarks to his interviewer in **Shielding the Flame** in 1977:

> Listen... Do you have any idea what bread meant at that time in the Ghetto? Because if you don't, you will never understand how thousands of people could voluntarily come for the bread and go on with this bread to the camp at Treblinka. Nobody has understood it thus far.[17]

Starvation sapped the will of the Ghetto population. But the demoralisation and despair had another source. The Jewish Councils and the Jewish Police, which the Nazis used to control the ghettos, knew about Nazi intentions and did nothing. Edelman describes how on the second day of the deportations to Treblinka, 22 July 1942, Adam Czerniakow, president of the Jewish Council, committed suicide. As Edelman says simply:

> He knew beyond doubt... he had no right to act as he did... It was his duty to inform the entire population of the real state of affairs and dissolve all public institutions, particularly the Jewish Police.[18]

The allegation in recent years that a strand within Zionism itself might have provided the moral and political justification for the inertia of the Jewish Councils sparked a furious controversy. This is a difficult subject. Yet the most recent

Jewish scholarship, describing the meeting in the Warsaw Ghetto, on the eve of the deportations, which rejected resistance to the Nazis, provides just the kind of evidence that has given the controversy its resonance:

> Dr Ignacy Schipper, historian and veteran Zionist activist... invited the assembled leaders to study the lessons of Jewish history: more than once the Jewish people had been forced to resign itself to cruel bloodletting in order to save the core of the nation and perpetuate Jewish existence.[19]

That peculiar Zionist fatalism, the idea that Jewish blood might have to be spilled in order to 'save' the Jewish nation, acted as a fog to obscure the behaviour of the Jewish Police who, in the words of a diarist of the Ghetto, were 'already known for their terrible corruption, but reached the apogee of depravity at the time of the deportation.'[20] It was the Jewish Police who helped the Nazis fill the cattle trucks.

From the beginning the Bund, the Jewish Socialist Party, had called for resistance. The left Zionist youth organisations, Hashomer and Hechalutz, and the newly re-formed Communist Party agreed, but attempts to form a joint battle organisation between them in February 1942 failed. Lack of trust, rooted in pre-war hostilities between these organisations, prevented a military pact and hence no united resistance was formed. Everyone who wanted to fight knew that the inclusion of the Bund in any battle organisation 'was vital both because of its influence within the Jewish underground and its status and ties with the Polish Underground.'[21]

These ties had helped provide the Bund with the first hard evidence that the deportations led to the death camps, when a Bund member secretly followed the trains with the help of a railworker who was a member of the Polish Socialists. The Bund released the truth to the Ghetto in its underground paper **On Guard**, but the Ghetto refused to believe it. The Ghetto was at this point effectively leaderless and it sank to its saddest state. Edelman's descriptions of this time are unbearable to read.

Meanwhile the Bund had tried to arm its own battle organisation through its contacts in the Polish Socialist Party outside the Ghetto, but had failed. There are depressing references to members of the Bund waiting for guns that never arrived.

Because of this, some have accused the Bund of underestimating the degree of anti-semitism that affected the Polish Underground. A more likely explanation, however, is that the Bund's isolation inside the Ghetto led it to underestimate the destruction of the left wrought by the Nazi-Soviet occupation. Hitler had Polish Socialist Party members executed. Stalin had them deported to Siberia. Stalin also had surviving members of the Bund executed, most notoriously the Bund leaders Erlich and Alter in 1941. Under the impact of these attacks, the Polish Socialist Party split: the resulting right faction *was* unfortunately open to anti-semitic influence, but the left faction—who continued to call themselves the Polish Socialists—was not. It did its best to assist the Bund, though it too was short of weapons.

The Nazis ended the first wave of 'deportations' in September 1942. The decimation had been catastrophic. Two-thirds of the Ghetto population had been 'removed', leaving a remnant of about 60,000 people. Emmanuel Ringelblum, the revered diarist of the Ghetto, recorded the feelings of the survivors. By October 1942, he tells us:

> the majority of Jews understood what a terrible mistake had been committed by not resisting the SS... if everybody had attacked the Germans with knives, clubs, shovels, choppers; if we had received the Germans, Ukrainians, Latvians and the Jewish Ghetto Police with acid, molten pitch, boiling water and so on—to put it in a nutshell, if men, women and children, the young and the old, had risen in a single people's levy, there would not have been 350,000 murdered at Treblinka, but only 50,000 shot dead in the streets of Warsaw. Men tore their hair out at the thought that they had allowed their nearest and dearest to be hauled away with impunity; children reproached

themselves aloud that they had allowed their parents to be carted away...[22]

This resistance was exactly what the Bund had called for at the start of the deportations, when it had issued a leaflet saying: 'Don't let them snatch you. Defend yourselves even if only with bare hands...'[23]

Ringelblum concluded:

> The oath sworn over the heads of the victims was kept. The Ghetto began to arm itself.[24]

The moment of truth had arrived. The political organisations willing to stand by this oath came together to form the Jewish Resistance Organisation—in Polish, *Zydowska Organizacja Bojowa,* usually referred to as the ZOB. The ZOB incorporated those organisations that were now willing literally to fight to the death: the main Zionist organisations, the Communist Party and the Bund. One of its first tasks was to locate responsibility for the failure to fight so far:

> The monumental betrayal of the Warsaw Judenrat [the Jewish Council]... which consisted in completely ignoring or pretending to ignore the real situation, will forever remain, next to the betrayal of the Ghetto Police, an unremovable stain on the Jewish Ghetto authority...[25]

Avenging this betrayal was seen as a prime way of beginning to galvanise what remained of the Ghetto into action. In fact the left Zionists and the Communists in the Anti-Fascist Block had already carried out an attempted assassination of the Jewish Police chief, Szerynski. This had triggered a change in the atmosphere in the Ghetto. News of spontaneous resistance, such as the Jew who 'flung himself on a German and tried to throttle him', and another who 'had wrenched a rifle from the hands of a Ukrainian soldier and had run away with it', spread like wildfire.[26]

The Bund was in a very poor state. It had been savagely hit by the 'deportations', losing the majority of its members. Those who survived threw themselves into the ZOB with tremendous enthusiasm. Edelman himself became one of its key commanders.

On 29 October 1942 the ZOB carried out its first major action by successfully assassinating Jacob Lejkin, Szerynski's deputy commander of the Jewish Police. One month later they killed Israel First, the notorious liaison man between the Gestapo and the Judenrat. Both acts were in line with the declared policy of eliminating Jewish traitors and collaborators as a means of establishing the ZOB as the principal authority in the Ghetto.

Then, on 18 January 1943, the Nazis surrounded the Ghetto for the final liquidation. The Warsaw Ghetto uprising was about to begin.

The last part of **The Ghetto fights** is glorious. Edelman's description of the uprising is a monument to the kind of courage which is beyond the imagination of most of us. It remains as proof that defiance can come to the most downtrodden and humiliated. For the remnant of the Warsaw Ghetto did momentarily bring the Nazi death machine to a halt.

The Ghetto fighters forced the Nazis to fight their biggest battle on Polish soil since 1939, a potential spark for wider Polish resistance. On 1 May 1943 the Nazi propaganda chief Josef Goebbels wrote in his diary:

> The Jews have actually succeeded in making a defensive position of the Ghetto. Heavy engagements are being fought... it shows what is to be expected of the Jews when they are in possession of arms. Unfortunately some of their weapons are good German ones. Heaven only knows where they got them from.[27]

The finest epitaph to the Ghetto fighters was written by one of the leaders of the Polish Underground Rising of 1944. In a paper entitled 'The Military Importance of the April Uprising', General Jerzy Kirchmayer wrote that the Ghetto Uprising in Warsaw,

> the largest resistance centre during the Nazi occupation, was of a special nature insofar as it was staged by the

Jewish population, that is, by the population that was supposed to be absolutely incapable of any active, let alone armed, resistance. The blows delivered by the Jewish fighters hurt badly the prestige of General Stroop's 'heroes' [Stroop was the Nazi commander responsible for the Ghetto], who, although armed to the teeth, were forced to bring in tanks, artillery and planes against insurgents who were almost completely devoid of arms... The Warsaw Ghetto fell after a heroic fight but the idea of armed struggle... reached beyond the walls, survived and endured... It was carried abroad by the few Jews who reached the forests and fought there... It was spread by Poles who in Warsaw saw Nazis unsuccessfully attempting to break the resistance of the few and almost weaponless ZOB groups...

The momentary successes of the insurgents toppled the Germans from their pedestal of omnipotence and proved to Poles the effectiveness of armed resistance. Thus the blood of the Ghetto fighters was not shed in vain. It gave birth to the intensified struggle against the fascist invader and from this struggle there came victory.[28]

5.

Many modern historians of the Warsaw Ghetto[29] have persisted with the argument that the Polish Underground, led by the Polish 'Home Army' (in Polish, *Armia Krajowa* or AK), did have enough weapons but would not release them to the Ghetto fighters. They identify anti-semitism as the reason for this. At the same time, general histories of wartime Poland suggest that AK was appallingly short of heavy weapons even at the time of the nationwide uprising against the Nazis in 1944, when arms supplies from the Allies were much easier to obtain.[30]

There is a further consideration. AK was led by the Polish right, nationalist and conservative generals and politicians, some of them undoubtedly prone to the anti-semitic mythology that had dominated Polish ruling circles before the war. This situation was unusual. The liberation forces elsewhere in

Nazi-occupied Europe were organised around the workers' movements, led by the local Communist parties. Why was the Polish Communist Party so feeble?

While it is true that all Europe's Communist parties had felt the paralysing hand of Stalin's sudden and cynical switches in foreign policy, none felt these so acutely as that in Poland. The party there had been directly liquidated by Stalin and hundreds of its leading members executed in anticipation of the Hitler-Stalin Pact just before the war. Thus the situation in Poland concentrated the twentieth century's crisis of Communism in its most extreme form: Communism, supposedly the expression of working-class aspirations and the real counterweight to Nazism, was metamorphosised as a monster, devouring its own children in order to clear the path for Hitler's death march into Poland in 1939.

The Polish Communist Party was re-formed with Stalin's agreement after Hitler invaded Russia in 1941. It faced a hopeless task: to become a mass party and the backbone of resistance to the Nazis. The party was all too obviously an agent of a feared foreign power, whatever the intentions of many courageous individual Polish communists. The AK leadership was easily able to exclude the Polish Communist militia from its ranks. The remnants of the Polish Socialist Party struggled as best they could, but never recovered the strength they had had before the war.

Coincidentally as the battles raged in the Warsaw Ghetto in April 1943, General Sikorski, as head of the Polish government-in-exile in London, was told of the discovery of the bodies of thousands of Polish officers, slaughtered on Stalin's orders, in the forests of Katyn. The repercussions of the Katyn massacre rumble on to this day. Katyn symbolised for the Poles the bloody oppression they had experienced already at the hands of Stalin. Sikorski's preoccupation with Katyn was used to justify his delay in issuing a clear declaration to the Polish people to support the Ghetto fighters.

Katyn also burst the tentative alliance between AK and the Russian Red Army and elevated 'anti-Communism' once again to a major plank in Polish policy. AK's suspicions turned out to be justified. During the 1944 rising, Stalin held the Red Army back outside Warsaw until the Nazis had crushed the Polish resistance fighters and razed the city to the ground.

Of course Katyn does not at all excuse Sikorski for delaying support for the Ghetto fighters. But it illustrates well the difficulty the left had in overcoming the heavy presence of Stalinism, which constantly handed advantages to the right.

Setting such considerations aside, could the Polish Underground have provided the heavy weapons that the Ghetto fighters so desperately needed? Edelman insists that they could not:

> It must be taken into account that the time was the year 1942. The resistance movement of the Poles was just beginning at the time, and only vague stories were being circulated about partisans in the woods. It must be remembered that the first organised act of armed resistance on the part of the Poles did not take place until March 1943. Therefore, there was nothing unusual in the fact that our efforts to obtain arms and ammunition... encountered major difficulties.[31]

The Ghetto fights was published in 1945. The heat of the battle had hardly died away. Perhaps in the many years he has had to reflect on this matter he has reconsidered his point of view. I put this to him when I interviewed him in 1989. This was his reply:

> Naturally I uphold what I wrote. The situation was very difficult. The Polish resistance thought that the uprising was premature. The Ghetto rising started the general rising of the Polish resistance. The Polish resistance thought that the front was so far away. The Polish leaders were afraid that the Ghetto rising might also destroy Warsaw. The Polish army was itself poorly equipped. It was hard to convince them, but they still gave us the guns. The uprising was doomed to fail. It was more a symbolic gesture to make the world recognise us.

I then asked him why, nonetheless, the view had persisted that anti-semitism held back the guns from the Ghetto. He replied:

> There were nationalistic formations in the resistance that
> were anti-semitic, organisations that wanted to resettle
> the Jews. In the church there were also very strong
> influences of this nationalistic kind. But there were also
> different attitudes: many who wanted to help the Jews.[32]

The ZOB knew that their fight was not exclusively a Jewish
struggle, but part of a wider struggle for liberation from the
Nazis. The remarkable thing about these Jewish socialists is
that, despite all the terrible atrocities that they had witnessed
imposed on their comrades, friends and families, their belief in
a basic internationalism did not waver. In the days of the
uprising, in April 1943, the ZOB issued their 'Manifesto to the
Poles', which must rank as one of the greatest socialist appeals
of the twentieth century:

> Poles, citizens, soldiers of Freedom! Through the din of
> German cannon, destroying the homes of our mothers,
> wives and children: through the noise of their
> machine-guns, seized by us in the fight against the
> cowardly German police and SS men; through the smoke
> of the Ghetto, that was set on fire, and the blood of its
> mercilessly killed defenders, we, the slaves of the Ghetto,
> convey heartfelt greetings to you.
> We are well aware that you have been witnessing
> breathlessly, with broken hearts, with tears of
> compassion, with horror and enthusiasm, the war that we
> have been waging against every brutal occupant these past
> few days.
> Every doorstep in the Ghetto has become a stronghold and
> shall remain a fortress until the end! All of us will probably
> perish in the fight, but we shall never surrender! We, as
> well as you, are burning with the desire to punish the
> enemy for all his crimes, with a desire for vengeance. It is
> a fight for our freedom, as well as yours; for our human
> dignity and national honour, as well as yours! We shall
> avenge the gory deeds of Oswiecim, Treblinka, Belzec and

Majdanek!
Long live the fraternity of blood and weapons in a fighting
Poland!
Long live freedom!
Death to the hangmen and the killer!
We must continue our mutual struggle against the
occupant until the very end!
—*Jewish Armed Resistance Organisation*[33]

Editor's note on the text

These documents about the Warsaw Ghetto, particularly those in the appendices, were clearly written in difficult circumstances. As a result they contain inconsistencies. Names are frequently given in different ways even where it is clear that the references are to one and the same person. Sometimes it is not. The names of streets within the ghetto are sometimes given their Polish spelling ('Umszlag Platz'), sometimes German ('Umschlagplatz'). In the circumstances, any attempt to clear up these inconsistencies might have led to the introduction of unintentional inaccuracies. Therefore while obvious spelling errors have been corrected, any inconsistencies in the text have been left as they appeared in the original edition.

Notes were added to the text by the editors of the 1945 edition. These too have been left as originally published, and appear in square brackets in the text. The editors of this 1990 edition have kept their own textual notes to a minimum, attempting only to elucidate references that the passage of almost 50 years may have rendered unclear to an English readership.

The Ghetto fights
Marek Edelman

Dedicated to the memory of Abrasha Blum

The Ghetto fights

WHEN THE GERMANS occupied Warsaw in 1939, they found the Jewish political and social world in a state of complete chaos and disintegration. Almost all the leading personalities had left Warsaw on 7 September.[1] The 300,000 Jews there experienced a deeper feeling of loneliness and helplessness than the others.

In such conditions it was easy for the Germans to dominate the population from the very beginning by breaking their spirit through persecutions and by evoking a state of passive submission in their midst. The experienced and devilishly refined German propaganda agencies worked ceaselessly to achieve these aims, spreading incredible—for those days—rumours which further increased the panic and derangement in Jewish life. Then, after a short period of time, the maltreatment of Jews passed the stage of an occasional punch in the nose, sadistic extractions of Jews from their homes, and chaotic nabbing of Jews in the streets for aimless work.[2] The persecutions now became definite and systematic.

As early as November, 1939, the first 'exterminating' decrees were made public: the establishment of 'educational' camps for the Jewish population as a whole, and the appropriation of all Jewish assets in excess of 2,000 zloty per family. Later, one after another, a multitude of prohibitive rules and ordinances appeared. Jews were forbidden to work in key industries, in government institutions, to bake bread, to earn more than 500 zloty a month (and the price of bread rose, at times, to as high as 40 zloty a pound), to buy from or sell to

'Aryans',[3] to seek comfort at 'Aryan' doctors' offices, to doctor 'Aryan' sick, to ride on trains and trolley-cars, to leave the city limits without special permits, to possess gold or jewellery, and so on. After 12 November, every Jew twelve years of age or older was compelled to wear on his right arm a white arm-band with the blue Star of David printed on it (in certain cities, for example Lodz and Wloclawek, yellow signs on the back and chest).

The Jews—beaten, stepped upon, slaughtered without the slightest cause—lived in constant fear. There was only one punishment for failure to obey regulations—death—while careful obedience of the rules did not protect against a thousand more and more fantastic degradations, more and more acute persecutions, recurrent acts of terror, more far-reaching regulations. To top it all, the unwritten law of common responsibility was being universally applied against the Jews. Thus, in the first days of November, 1939, 53 male inhabitants of the 9 Nalewki Street apartment house were summarily shot for the beating of a Polish policeman by one of the tenants. This occurrence, the first case of mass punishment, intensified the feeling of panic amongst the Warsaw Jews. Their fear of the Germans now took on unequalled forms.

In this atmosphere of terror and fear, and under conditions cardinally changed, the Bund resumed—or, to be more specific, continued—its political and social activities. The Bund was the largest Jewish party in Poland, and was founded in 1897. Its programme was socialist, and it was in strong opposition to the pre-war Polish government.[4] Despite everything that was happening, there were among us, it seemed, people ready to attempt further work. First, psychological difficulties had to be overcome. For instance, a strongly depressing handicap was the feeling that one could perish momentarily *not* as a result of one's particular work, but as a beaten and humiliated—not human being—but Jew.

This conviction that one was never treated as an individual human being caused a lack of self-confidence and stunted the desire to work. These factors will perhaps best explain why our activities in the first period after the fall of Warsaw were mainly of a charitable nature, and why the first instinctive acts of armed resistance against the occupying forces occurred comparatively late and, in the beginning, in such insignificant forms. To overcome our own terrifying apathy, to force ourselves to the smallest spark of activity, to fight against our own acceptance of the generally prevailing feeling of panic—even these small tasks required truly gigantic efforts on our part.

Even during our darkest moments, the Bund did not suspend its activities for the shortest time. When the party's central committee was forced to leave the city in September, 1939, it had placed the responsibility of continuing the political activities of the Bund in the hands of Abrasha Blu... He, together with Szmul Zygielbojm and in cooperation with the efforts of Warsaw's mayor, Starzynski, organised Jewish detachments which took an active part in the defence of the capital. Almost the entire editorial staff of the **Folkszajtung** (**The People's Gazette**—the party daily) had left. However, the publication of the **Folkszajtung** was continued. During the siege period it appeared regularly, edited by Victor Szulman, Szmul Zygielbojm and others.

Public kitchens and canteens originated during the siege continued their activities after the seizure of the city. Almost all party and trade union members received financial help. Immediately following the arrival of the Germans, the new central bureau of the party was organised (A Blum, L Klog, Mrs S Nowogrodzki, B Goldsztejn, S Zygielbojm, later A Sznajdmil ('Berek') and M Orzech).

In January, 1940, after the first radio transmitting station of the Polish Underground had been found by the Germans, a new wave of mass-terror commenced. During a single night the Germans arrested and murdered over 300 people comprising social leaders, intelligentsia and professionals. This was not all. The so-called '*Seuchensperrgebiet*' (area threatened by typhus) was established, and Jews were forbidden to live outside of this designated area. Furthermore, the Jews were being forced to work for both German and Polish employers, and were generally looked upon as a source of cheap labour. This did not suffice either. The world was to be shown that the Jews were hated not only by the Germans.

Thus, during the Easter holidays of 1940, pogroms lasting several days were instigated. The German Air Corps engaged Polish hoodlums for four *zloty* per 'working day'. The first three days the hooligans raged unopposed. On the fourth day the Bund militia carried out revenge actions. Four major street battles resulted in the following localities: Solna Street-Mirowski Market Square, Krochmalna Street-Grzybowski Square, Karmelicka Street-Nowolipie Street., and Niska Street-Zamenhof Street. Comrade Bernard Goldsztejn commanded all of these battles from his hide-out.

The fact that none of the other active political parties took part in this action is significant as an example of the utter misconception of existing conditions common to Jewish groups at the time. All other groups even opposed our action. It was, however, our determined stand that momentarily checked the Germans' activities and went on record as the first Jewish act of resistance.

It was imperative that the public understand the significance of the events. It was imperative that all the beaten, maltreated people be told and shown that despite all we were still able to raise our heads. This was the immediate purpose of the first issue of **The Bulletin** which appeared for May Day, published on the battered Skif mimeograph machine which had been found by chance in the public school at 29 Karmelicka Street.[5] The editorial committee included Abrasha Blum, Adam Sznajdmil and Bernard Goldsztejn. The entire issue was dedicated to an analysis of the Easter disturbances. It met, however, with indifference on the part of the public.

In November, 1940, the Germans finally established the Warsaw Ghetto. The Jewish population still living outside the 'Seuchensperrgebiet' was brought inside the special area. Poles living within the designated Ghetto boundaries were ordered to move out. Small factories , shops and stores were allowed two weeks more, until 1 December, to complete their evacuation. But, beginning with 15 November, no Jew was allowed to leave the Jewish precincts. All houses vacated by

Jews were immediately locked by the Germans and then, with all their contents, gratuitously given to Polish merchants and hucksters. Hucksters and small-time pedlars, the typical brood of war conditions, those were the people upon whom the Germans counted, whose favours they tried to gain by presenting them with confiscated Jewish assets and by tolerating their practice of food-smuggling.

The walls and barbed wire surrounding the Ghetto grew higher every day until, on 15 November, they completely cut off the Jews from the outside world. Contacts with Jews living in other cities and towns were, naturally, also made impossible. For Jewish workers, all possibilities to earn a living vanished. Not only all factory workers, but all those who had been working in 'Aryan' enterprises, as well as government agencies, became unemployed. The typically wartime group of 'middlemen', tradesmen appeared. The great majority, however, left jobless, started selling everything that could possibly be sold, and slowly approached the depths of extreme poverty. The Germans, it is true, widely publicised their policy of 'increasing the productive power of the Ghetto', but actually they achieved the complete pauperisation of the population. The Ghetto population was increased by thousands of Jews evicted from neighbouring towns. These people with practically nothing to their names, alone, in strange surroundings where others were preoccupied with their own difficulties, literally dying of malnutrition, tried to build their existence anew.

The complete segregation of the Ghetto, the regulations under which no newspaper could be brought into it and all the news from the outside world carefully kept out, had a very definite purpose. These regulations contributed to the development of a special way of thinking common to the Ghetto inhabitants. Everything taking place outside the Ghetto walls became more and more foggy, distant, strange. Only the present day really mattered. Only matters of the most personal nature, the closest family circle of friends were by now the focal point of interest of the average Ghetto inhabitant. The most important thing was simply 'to be alive'.

This 'life' itself, however, had a different meaning to each, depending on his environment and opportunities. It was a life of plenty for the still-wealthy few, it was exuberant and colourful for a variety of depraved Gestapo men and demoralised smugglers, and, for a multitude of workers and unemployed, it was a hungry existence upheld by the meagre public kitchens' soup and rationed bread. Everyone tried to hang on to his particular sort of 'life' as best he could. Those who had money sought the essence of their existence in comfortable living, strove to find it in the dense, chattery air of overcrowded cafés, or plunged into the dance music of the night clubs. Those who had nothing, the paupers, sought their 'happiness' in a rotten potato recovered from a garbage pit, found evasive joy in a piece of begged-for bread with which the taste of hunger could, for a while, be stilled. These were the tragic contrasts of the Ghetto so often exploited by the Germans, photographed for propaganda purposes and maliciously presented to the opinion of the world: 'In the Warsaw Ghetto beggars, swollen from hunger, die in front of luscious window displays of food smuggled from the "Aryan" sections...'

The hunger increased daily. From dark, overcrowded living quarters it got out into the streets, came into sight in the shape of ridiculously swollen, log-shaped bodies with diseased feet, covered with open wounds, wrapped in dirty rags. It spoke through the mouths of the beggars, the aged, the young, and the children, in the streets and courtyards.

Children begged everywhere, in the Ghetto as well as on the 'Aryan' side. Six-year-old boys crawled through the barbed wire under the very eyes of the gendarmes in order to obtain food 'on the other side'. They supported entire families in this manner. Often a lone shot in the vicinity of the barbed wire told the casual passers-by that another little smuggler had died in his fight with omnipotent hunger. A new 'profession' appeared, the so-called 'catchers'. Boys, or rather shadows of former boys, would snatch packages from pedestrians and immediately, while still running, devour the contents. In their haste, they sometimes stuffed themselves full of soap or uncooked peas...

Such was the misery by now that people began to die of hunger in the streets. Every morning, about 4-5am, funeral carts collected a dozen or more corpses on the streets that had been covered with a sheet of paper and weighted down with a few rocks. Some simply fell in the streets and remained there, others died in their own homes but their families, after having stripped them completely (in order to sell the clothes), dumped the bodies in front of the houses so that burial would be made at the cost of the Jewish Community Council. Cart after cart filled with nude corpses would move through the streets. One on top of the other the bony carcasses lay, the heads bobbing up and down and beating against one another or against the wood of the cart on the uneven pavement.

When the Ghetto was once more flooded with evicted Jews from smaller cities and towns, the situation became disastrous. There were never enough houses and living quarters. Now homeless, grimy people began loitering in the streets. All day long they camped in the courtyards, ate there, slept there, lived there. Finally, when there was no other way, they turned to the specially established 'points'—transient homes for refugees. These 'points' were one of the darkest spots of Ghetto life, a real plague with which it was virtually impossible to cope (only some of the children could be moved into children's homes, where conditions were better).

A few hundred people crowd every large, unheated room of a synagogue, every hall of a deserted factory. Unkempt, lousy, with no facilities to wash, undernourished, and hungry ('water soups' are given once daily by the Jewish Community Council), they remain all day on their filthy straw mattresses, with no strength to rise. The walls are green, slimy, mildewed. The mattresses usually lie on the ground, seldom on wooden supports. A whole family often receives sleeping space for one. This is the kingdom of hunger and misery.

*   *   *

Simultaneously spotted fever raged in the Ghetto. Yellow signs reading *'Fleckfieber!'* (Spotted Fever) were affixed to a constantly increasing number of doors and entrances. Particularly great numbers of the starvelings at the 'points' were afflicted. All hospitals, by now handling contagious diseases exclusively, were overcrowded. A hundred and fifty sick daily were being admitted to a single ward and placed two or three in a bed, or on the floors. The dying were viewed impatiently—let them vacate quicker for the next one! Physicians simply could not keep up with it. There hadn't been enough of them in the first place. Hundreds were dying at a given instance. The grave-diggers were unable to dig fast enough. Although hundreds of corpses were being put into every grave, hundreds more had to lie around for several days, filling the graveyard with a sickening, sweetish odour. The epidemic kept growing. It could not be controlled. Typhus was everywhere, and from everywhere it threatened. It shared mastery over the Ghetto with the overpowering hunger. The monthly mortality rate reached 6000 (over 2 per cent of the population).

In such tragic conditions, the Germans attempted to establish a semblance of law and order. The Jewish Council (*Judenrat*) officially governed the Ghetto from the very first day of its establishment. To secure 'order' a uniformed Jewish police force was formed. The children smuggling across the barbed wires now had to be careful lest still another official would catch them, and the Ghetto population received another Cerberus,[6] making a total of three: the Germans, the Polish policemen, and the Jewish policemen. But the agencies established to give the Ghetto a semblance of normal life were in reality nests of corruption and demoralisation. The Germans succeeded in drafting the best- known citizens into serving on the Jewish Council. The only member of the council, however, who threatened to leave that agency despite the death penalty for such an act was Comrade Arthur (Szmul Zygielbojm).

Such was life in the Ghetto when the first report of the

gassing of Jews in Chelmno, Pomerania, reached Warsaw. The news was brought by three persons who were to be put to death in Chelmno and who had miraculously escaped. Their story showed that during November and December, 1940, approximately 40,000 Jews from Lodz, another 40,000 from Pomerania and towns from other regions incorporated into the Reich, and also a few hundred Gypsies from Bessarabia, had died in the Chelmno gas-chambers. They had been murdered by the Germans in the now well-known vile manner. The victims were told they were being taken for work and ordered to take along hand-luggage. Upon their arrival at the Chelmno Castle they were stripped of all their clothes and everyone was given a towel and soap, supposedly for the bathing that was to follow. All appearances were kept up to the very last minute. The victims were led into hermetically closed trucks containing gas chambers. The gas was forced into the chambers by the truck engines. Afterwards, in a clearing in the woods in the vicinity of Chelmno, Jewish gravediggers unloaded the corpses from the trucks and buried them. The woods were surrounded by 200 SS-men. A certain SS-man called Bykowiec was in charge of the procedure. Inspections by SS and SA generals occurred several times.

The Warsaw Ghetto did not believe these reports. People who clung to their lives with superhuman determination were unable to believe that they could be killed in such a manner. Only our organised groups, carefully noting the steadily increasing signs of German terror, accepted the Chelmno story as indeed probable, and decided upon extensive propaganda activities in order to inform the population of the imminent danger. A meeting of the Zukunft *cadres*[7] took place in mid-February, 1941, with Abrasha Blum and Abramek Bortensztein as speakers. All of us agreed to offer resistance before being led to death. We were ashamed of the Chelmno Jews' submissiveness, of their failure to rise in their own defence. We did not want the Warsaw Ghetto ever to act in a similar way. 'We shall not die on our knees', said Abramek. 'Not they will be an example for us, but men like our comrade Alter Bas.' While Chelmno victims were dying passively and humbly he, after having been caught as a political leader, with illegal papers in his pocket, and tortured in every manner known to the Germans, resisted the barbarous torment through superhuman efforts, when but a few words would have saved his life.

A few dozen copies of a report on the Chelmno murders were circulated throughout the Ghetto. This report was also sent abroad, together with the demand to take retaliatory measures against the German civilian population. But public opinion abroad did not believe the story either. Our appeal found no response. Comrade Arthur Zygielbojm, our representative in the Polish National Council in London, broadcast the literal text of our message in a radio speech to the whole world a year later. The following morning his appeal was circulated in the Ghetto both in a special edition of our publication **Der Weker** and in the papers of all other political groups.

The beginning of the Russo-German war (summer, 1941) was also the time of extensive exterminating activities on the part of the Germans in the Western Ukrainian and White Russian territories. In November, 1941, the mass-shooting of Jews in Wilno, Slonim, Bialystok, and Baranowicze occurred. In Ponary (near Wilno) tens of thousands of Jews perished in rapid killings. The news reached Warsaw, but the uninformed public again took a near-sighted view of the situation. The majority was still of the opinion that the murders were not a result of an organised, orderly policy to exterminate the Jewish people, but acts of misbehaviour on the part of victory-drunk troops. Political parties, however, were now beginning to understand the true state of affairs.

In January, 1942, an inter-party conference was called. By now all parties agreed that armed resistance was the only appropriate answer to the persecutions. The Hashomer and Hechalutz organisations[8] for the first time suggested a plan for a mutual battle organisation. Maurycy Orzech and Abrasha Blum addressed the conference on behalf of our movement, maintaining that an armed uprising could be successful only if carried out in agreement with the Polish Underground and with their cooperation. However, the common battle organisation was not established at that time.

It was our group that called the first battle organisation into being with the knowledge of the Polish Socialists.[9] Bernard Goldsztejn, Abrasha Blum, and Berek Szmajdmil constituted the Command. The first 'five' of instructors[10] was organised and comprised Liebeskind (from Lodz), Zygmunt Frydrych, Lejb Szpichler, Abram Fajner, Marek Edelman. We started work with theoretical instruction, but the complete lack of weapons made it impossible to broaden our activities. Thus we were practically limited in our activities to intelligence work among the Germans and, in close relation to the foregoing, the warning of particular people against possible 'slip-ups'. The following people were active in our intelligence service: Pola Lipszyc, Cywia Waks, Zoska Goldblat, Lajcia Blank, Stefa Moryc, Mania Elenbogen, comrades from the Polish Socialist Party: Marian Meremholc, Mietek Dab, and others. Despite our very limited possibilities, the mere fact of establishing such an organisation was of obvious importance. Our initiative met with the full approval of all those in the know.

In those days the Bund was quite a large organisation, considering the clandestine working conditions. More than 2000 people participated in the festivities occasioned by the Bund's 44th anniversary in October, 1941. These meetings were held in many places simultaneously. On the surface nothing was discernible, and it was difficult to realise how great the number of small groups—dispersed 'fives' or 'sevens' meeting in private apartments—really was.

The Central Trade Union Council was also revived (Bernard Goldsztejn, Kersz, Mermelsztein), and eventually registered approximately 30,000 former union members.

The scope of the Zukunft's work was also quite extensive. The clandestine Zukunft Committee established itself during the first days of October, 1939, and by mid-November, 1939, the first 'fives' were meeting. In the generally tragic conditions of Jewish life, the lot of Jewish youth was the worst. Young Jews were being persecuted by the Germans with special cruelty. These young men, whom the Germans continuously hunted for forced labour, were not even free to walk the streets, let alone attempt regular work. To remedy their difficulties, the Zukunft established cooperative enterprises where young people could find employment. In 1940 two barber shops were opened, a cooperative tailor shop, and a cooperative shoemaker shop. The shops served not only as working places, but as comparatively safe meeting places for the entire organisation as well. It was here that the first *Zukunftsturm* (Zukunft Militia) met. With the increase in the scope of work, the Zukunft and Skif Committees merged into one (Henoch Russ, Abramek Bortensztein, Lejb Szpichler, Mojszele Kaufman, Rywka Rozensztajn, Fajgele Peltel, Welwl Rozowski, Jankiel Gruszka, Szlojme Paw, Marek Edelman).

In 1941 a Youth Division was established at the Jewish Social Mutual Aid Organisation and the Zukunft became one of the division's important contributors. We were able to reach large numbers of young people. Our lecturers took charge of numerous youth groups, which were at that time established under the House Committees in every apartment house. There was the choir with its active program (public concerts were given in the Judaistic Library). School-aged youth was also being organised. The SOMS (Socialist School Students' Organisation) was re-established, and numbered a few hundred members after a very short time. Comprehensive political education and cultural activities were carried out.

At the same time the Skif, whose activities were until then limited to securing financial help for its pre-war members, started large-scale work among children of school and pre-school ages. A so-called 'corner' was established in every house, where children found a home for a few hours every day. The Dramatic Club, led by Pola Lipszyc, gave performances every week. During the 1941 season 12,000 children attended these performances (**Dolls** and **The Granary**[11] were shown 80 times). Instruction classes were held for children 12-15 years of age. The Instructors' Council members themselves attended instruction classes covering a full secondary school course.

Six periodicals were published by us in those days: 1. **Der**

Weker (weekly), 2. **The Bulletin** (monthly), 3. *Tsait Fragn* ('Problems of the Times'—a theoretical political magazine), 4. **For Our and Your Freedom** (monthly), 5. *Yugnt Shtime* ('The Voice of Youth'—monthly), 6. **The New Youth** (monthly). Considerable effort went into the publication of these papers. As a rule, the single old Skif mimeograph machine would be working the whole night through. Usually no electricity was available, and working by carbide gas lights proved extremely strenuous. At about 2am the printing personnel (Rozowski, Zyferman, Blumka Klog, Marek) would complain of tremendous eye pains and it would be almost impossible to continue working. On the other hand, every minute was precious. At 7am the issue, no matter how many pages it held, had to be ready for circulation. Everyone worked harder than they were physically able to. They averaged two to three sleepless nights a week. It was impossible to catch up on one's sleep the following morning, because one had to pretend complete ignorance of the printing activities. The manager of the printing office, Marek, was also in charge of circulation (people actually circulating the paper were: Zoska Goldblat, Anka Wolkowicz, Stefa Moryc, Miriam Szyfman, Marynka Segalewicz, Cluwa Krysztal-Nisenbaum, Chajka Belchatowska, Halina Lipszyc and others. After a sleepless night, there usually followed a difficult day, always in suspense, uncertain whether everything reached its destination, whether all was in order, whether there were no 'slip-ups'.

Once Marynka was stopped in the street by a 'Navy-blue' (Polish) policeman while carrying 40 copies of **The Bulletin**. It happened under the Ghetto wall, on Franciszkanska Street. She pretended she was an 'ordinary' smuggler and wanted to take care of the matter accordingly—by offering a bribe of 500 *zloty*. The unusually high offer made the police suspicious, and they asked to be shown the 'merchandise'. Now the inevitable happened. Not stockings, but printed sheets of paper fell out from under the girl's shirt and littered the street. The matter became serious, and Marynka already saw herself in the Gestapo's dark shadow. Suddenly a lucky 'coincidence' occurred—an argument started not far away, and fists were soon flying. Such disturbances could not be tolerated near the Ghetto wall. The policemen lost their heads, did not know what to do first, and turned round for an instant—long enough for Marynka to gather the papers, throw the policemen their promised 500 *zloty*, and disappear... As to the 'argument', it was intentionally started by 'Little Kostek' (S Kostrynski), who had noticed Marynka's plight.

It might be interesting to add that according to a sort of poll that we were able to conduct, our publications were being read by an average of 20 people per copy.

Our periodicals were also circulated throughout the country. This phase of our work was organised by J Celemenski and I Falk, both of whom had been previously authorised by the Party Central Committee to maintain continuous contacts with groups throughout the country. In addition, Mendelson (Mendele) was delegated by the Zukunft Committee for the purpose of organising the work of youth groups outside Warsaw.

In the meantime the terror within the Ghetto kept increasing, while the Ghetto's isolation from the outside world became more and more rigid. More and more people were being arrested for sneaking on to the 'Aryan side', and finally 'special courts' were established. On 12 February, 1941, seventeen people previously sentenced to death for illegal trespassing in the 'Aryan section' lost their lives. The execution took place in the Jewish jail on Gesia Street. At 4am shrill cries notified the neighbourhood that 'justice' was being meted out, that seventeen outcasts, including four children and three women, were being duly punished for leaving the Ghetto in pursuit of a piece of bread or a few pennies. Cries from other jail cells could also be heard, the voices of future victims awaiting trial for the same offence, a total of 700 people. The same afternoon the entire Jewish population was notified of the execution by special posters signed by the German Commissar of the Ghetto, Dr Auerswald.

The Ghetto could clearly feel the breath of death.

During a short meeting of the Party Executive Committee

(Abrasha Blum, Luzer Klog, Berek Sznajdmil, Marek Orzech) held the same day, it was proposed to publish and post short leaflets reading: 'Shame to the Murderers'.

The Ghetto was dumbfounded by the terror of what was happening and by fear of large-scale retaliations on the part of the Germans. Once more every effort to decide on armed resistance was nipped in the bud. The fear of the Germans and of their policy of common responsibility was such that even the best refused to show any signs of protest.

Now the events began moving at a breathtaking pace. The Ghetto streets became a bloody slaughterhouse. The Germans made it a habit to shoot passers-by without the slightest provocation. People were afraid to leave their homes, but German bullets reached them through the windows. There were days when the toll of terror was 10-15 quite accidental victims. One of the more notorious sadists, a gendarme of the *Schutzpolizei*[12] by the name of Frankenstein, had on his conscience over 300 murdered people, more than half of whom were children.

Simultaneously, man-hunts were being conducted on the streets by German and Jewish Police. The captives were sent to various working camps throughout the General Government.[13] The Germans gained doubly from that procedure: first, they obtained the needed working power; secondly, they were able to show that all evictions were caused by the Germans' desire to 'increase the productive power', and that in German working camps, even though the conditions were difficult, one had an opportunity to live through the war... The Germans were truly magnanimous. They even permitted the people to write to their families...

These letters found their way to the Ghetto in great numbers and their result was disbelief of the more and more persistent reports concerning mass-executions of Jews. Repeated deportations throughout the country, allegedly to Bessarabia, passed almost unnoticed, because the Ghetto obstinately believed the rumours that letters had arrived from these people also. Likewise, people dismissed as untrue the story of the wholesale slaughter of almost the entire transport of German Jews brought the previous year to the vicinity of Lublin. The stories about the executions in the Lublin woods were too horrible, it was thought, to be true.

The Ghetto did not believe.

We, however, did our utmost to obtain arms from the 'Aryan side'. We enlarged our battle organisation, whose members were mostly Bund youth *cadres* (Szmul Kostrynski, Jurek Blones, Janek Bilak, Lejb Rozensztajn, Icl Szpilberg, Kuba Zylberberg, Mania Elenbogen, and many others). It is difficult to describe here the manner and handicaps of our work. It was an unbroken chain of disappointments and failures. Repeatedly disappointing difficulties in securing weapons, lack of understanding for our efforts on the part of our Polish comrades—these were the conditions in which our group worked and grew.

At one point it looked as if we were about to attain our aim, and that transports of arms would soon start arriving in the Ghetto. Instead, news came about the liquidation of the Lublin Ghetto. Since a few months before, when the serious 'slip-up' of Celek and many others in Piotrkow and Lublin took place, communications with the groups outside the Ghetto were almost non-existent. The Warsaw Ghetto, lacking direct contacts with the outside, received these latest reports with scepticism too. People gave many reasons to refute the remotest possibility of similar acts of violence, refused to accept the thought that a similar murder could possibly be committed in Poland's capital where 300,000 Jews dwelled. People argued with one another and tried to convince others and themselves that 'even the Germans would not murder hundreds of thousands of people without any reason whatever, particularly in times when they were in such need of productive power...' A normal human being with normal mental processes was simply unable to conceive that a difference in the colour of eyes or hair or a different racial origin might be sufficient causes for murder.

However, immediately after the arrival of these reports came tragic and bloody events of the night of 17 April, 1942, like an omen of things to come. Over fifty social workers were dragged from their homes that night by German soldiers and shot in the Ghetto streets. Of our comrades we then lost Goldberg (the barber) and his wife, Naftali Leruch and his father, Sklar, and others. Sonia Nowogrodzka, Luzer Klog, and Berenbaum were also hunted by the Germans. The following morning the entire Ghetto, stunned, terrified, hysterical, tried to find reasons behind these executions. The majority came to the conclusion that the action was aimed at editors of clandestine papers, and that all illegal activities should have been stopped so as not to needlessly increase the tremendous number of victims.

On 19 April, a special edition of our weekly **Der Weker** was published, in which we tried to explain that the latest executions were but another link in the systematic policy of extermination practised against the Jews as a whole, and that the Germans wanted to get the Jewish population's more active elements out of the way. Once this was accomplished, the paper argued, the Germans hoped that the remaining masses would meekly accept their lot as they did in Wilno, Bialystok, Lublin and other cities. Our view, however, remained as isolated as it had been before. Only some youth groups, such as Hashomer and Hechalutz, shared our convictions.

At this time a complete reorganisation of our work took place. All our clandestine activities, we decided, would now be carried out with a single view in mind: to prepare our resistance. To expedite matters the Party Executive Committee was re-established (Abrasha Blum, Berek Szmajdmil, Marek Orzech). All youth 'fives' received basic military training. Special orders were issued. A detailed plan of action was worked out in the event of a German attempt to overrun the Ghetto. A transport of weapons promised by the Polish Socialists was to arrive shortly and was to comprise a hundred pistols and a few dozen rifles and grenades.

In the meantime our number decreased as a result of continuous executions. From 18 April to 22 July, 1942, the Germans killed between ten and fifteen Ghetto inhabitants per night. None of our comrades slept at home during that period. It was, however, very difficult to predict the Germans' intentions at any given time since they employed an involved pattern in choosing their victims. These stemmed from all social groups—smugglers, merchants, workers, professionals, etc. The purpose behind it was to implant fear among the population to such a degree as to render it incapable of any instinctive or organised actions, to cause the fear of death from the Germans to paralyse even the smallest acts of the people's resistance and to force them on to a path of blind, passive subordination. This, however, was clear to a small handful only. The Ghetto as a whole was unable to grasp the true reasons behind the German acts of terror.

It is difficult to relate today life in the Ghetto during those days preceding the 'official' exterminating procedure applied to its inhabitants. Now the sadistic and beastly methods of the Germans are well known to the world. A few examples of everyday happenings will suffice.

* * *

Three children sit, one behind the other, in front of the Bersons and Baumans hospital. A gendarme, passing by, shoots all three with a single round.

A pregnant woman trips and falls while crossing the street. A German, present during the accident, does not allow her to rise and shoots her there and then.

Dozens of those smuggling across the Ghetto Wall are killed by a new German technique: Germans clad in civilian clothes, with Jewish arm-bands and weapons hidden in burlap bags, wait for the instant when the smugglers scale the Wall. At that very moment machine pistols appear from the bags and the fate of the group is settled.

Every morning a small Opel (German-type car) stops at Orla street. Every morning a shackled man is thrown out of the car and shot in the first house entrance. It is a Jew who had been caught on the 'Aryan side' without identification papers.

* * *

In mid-May, 1942, 110 prisoners of the so-called Central

Jail (*Gesiowka*), arrested for illegal crossing to the 'Aryan side', were executed. One of our comrades (Grylak) saw the prisoners being led out of the jail and into special trucks. Almost all of them walked meekly into the cars, when suddenly one woman found courage to show her protest. From the steps of the truck she shouted: 'I shall die, but your death will be much worse!' Special proclamations signed by Dr Auerswald informed the Ghetto of the 'just' punishment received by the 110 'criminals'.

At about this time another of our major 'slip-ups' occurred. The Germans discovered the apartment where our printing shop was installed. They did not find anybody there, however, because our intelligence service had known about the German order to search the house 24 hours beforehand and as a result we had ample time to move our paper supply, the mimeograph machine, and the typewriters to another safe place.

The mood of the Ghetto was now changing daily. The turning point in the Ghetto, however, was 18 April. Until that day, no matter how difficult life had been, the Ghetto inhabitants felt that their everyday life, the very foundations of their existence, were based on something stabilised and durable; that one could try to balance one's budget or make preparations for the winter. On 18 April the very basis of Ghetto life started to move from under people's feet. Every night, filled with the shrill, crisp sound of shots, was an illustration that the Ghetto had no foundations whatever, that it lived at the will of the Germans, that it was brittle and weak like a house built of playing cards. By now everybody understood that the Ghetto was to be liquidated, but nobody yet realised that its entire population was destined to die.

By mid-July the black clouds became thicker. Appearances were normal enough. Only 'unlikely' rumours began to circulate—about the arrival of the *'Umsiedlungskommando'* (Deportation Board), about the proposed deportation of 20,000, 40,000, 60,000 Ghetto inhabitants, about taking all jobless for fortification works, about leaving in Warsaw only those who were actually employed. These rumours, although still considered implausible, caused uneasiness, then panic.

Great numbers of people started looking for work, tried to obtain employment in factories and public offices. Ladies, who, until then, had been spending their days in cafés, overnight became hardworking seamstresses, menders, clerks. Some shops gave preference to those in possession of sewing machines. The price of sewing machines immediately rose. Although no definite information was forthcoming, people became more and more panicky and willingly started paying larger and larger sums for a chance to work. 'To obtain work' was, at that time, the only topic of conversation, the only thought. Everybody had to work! Those 'established' were happy—a load was off their minds. The 'unestablished'— uneasy, irritated—followed every lead which might bring them employment.

On 20 July the arrests began. Almost all the doctors of the Czyste Hospital were locked up in the Pawiak Prison, as were part of the Jewish Mutual Aid Committee's managing personnel and several Community Councilmen (among others, G Jaszunski). That the Ghetto would shortly be liquidated was obvious.

On 22 July, 1942, at 10am, German cars halted at the Jewish Council buildings. The *Umsiedlungsstab* members[14] entered the house. At a short meeting the Judenrat members were told the Germans' desire. It was really a simple matter: all 'unproductive' Jews were to be deported somewhere to the East. The Germans departed and another secret meeting took place. Not a single councilman stopped to consider the basic question—whether the Jewish Council should undertake to carry out the order at all. The secretary of the Jewish Council addressed the meeting: 'Gentlemen, before you pass to the technical means of executing the order, stop and think—should it be done?' But his advice was not heeded. There was no debate on the implications of the order, only on the matters of procedure for its execution.

The following morning large white posters signed by the Judenrat (the text of proclamation was dictated by *Oberscharführer* Hoefle) made it clear to the Jewish population that all, with the exception of those working for the Germans (here followed a carefully prepared list of all working places which the order did not concern), employees of the Jewish Council, and the ZSS (Jewish Mutual Aid), would have to leave Warsaw. The Jewish police was designated as the agency to execute the deportation order, and its Command was to keep in touch with the *Umsiedlungsstab*. Thus the Germans made the Jewish Council itself condemn over 300,000 Ghetto inhabitants to death.

On the first day of the deportation period 2000 prisoners of the Central Jail were sent out, together with a few hundred beggars and starvelings who had been caught in the streets.

In the afternoon a meeting of our 'instructors' five' took place. We decided that in view of the complete lack of weapons and, therefore, the impossibility of offering resistance, our activities should be directed at saving from deportation as many people as possible. We thought that contacts maintained by certain welfare organisations with people within the Jewish Police—the agency in charge of the deportation procedure—would prove helpful. However, even before the end of the meeting and before the final details had been worked out, we heard that the Germans and Ukrainians themselves surrounded the Muranowska Street-Niska Street block, that they were attending to the 'technical details' themselves, and that they had already taken from these buildings 2000 people, the number lacking to fill the daily quota. (This quota was, in the first days of the deportation, 6000 people per day). According to this report, the Germans took everybody without discrimination. Even those in possession of certificates from German places of employment had to come along (L Rozensztajn perished in this manner). In view of the new developments our plans seemed quite unrealistic.

On the second day, 23 July, a meeting of the so-called Workers' Committee took place. All political parties were represented on the committee. Our group, supported only by the Hechalutz and Hashomer organisation, called for active resistance. But public opinion was against us. The majority still thought such action provocative and maintained that if the required contingent of Jews could be delivered, the remainder of the Ghetto would be left in peace. The instinct for self-preservation finally drove the people into a state of mind permitting them to disregard the safety of others in order to save their own necks. True, nobody as yet believed that the deportation meant death. But the Germans had already succeeded in dividing the Jewish population into two distinct groups—those already condemned to die and those who still hoped to remain alive. Afterwards, step by step, the Germans succeeded in pitting these two groups one against another and occasionally caused some Jews to lead others to certain death in order to save their own skin.

During the first days of the 'actions', the Party Council sat in continuous session (Orzech, Abrasha Blum, Berek Sznajdmil, Sonia Nowogrodzka, Bernard Goldsztejn, Klog, Paw, Grylak, Mermelsztajn, Kersz, Wojland, Russ, Marek Edelman, and a comrade from the Polish Socialists). We were awaiting the arrival of weapons at any hour then. Our youth groups were all ready. For three days, until the time when all hopes to obtain the promised weapons had to be given up, a state of 'acute emergency' for our mobilised groups prevailed. All our other members were also mobilised and concentrated at several designated spots awaiting orders. Such was the feeling of excitement and apprehension that several street fights with members of the Jewish Police who were taking part in the 'action' took place.

On the second day of the 'deportations' the president of the Jewish Council, Adam Czerniakow, committed suicide. He knew beyond any doubt that the supposed 'deportation to the East' actually meant the death of hundreds and thousands of people in gas-chambers, and he refused to assume responsibility for it. Being unable to counteract events he decided to quit altogether. At the time, however, we thought that he had no right to act as he did. We thought that since he was the only person in the Ghetto whose voice carried a great deal of authority, it had been his duty to inform the entire population of the real state of affairs, and also to dissolve all public institutions, particularly the Jewish Police, which had been established by the Jewish Council and was legally subordinate to it.

The same day the first issue of our paper **On Guard**, in which we warned the population not to volunteer for deportation, and called for resistance, appeared. 'Utterly helpless as we are', Comrade Orzech wrote in the editorial, 'we must not let ourselves be caught. Fight against it with all means at your disposal!' This issue, published in three times the usual number of copies, was circulated throughout the Ghetto during the fourth and fifth days of the deportation action.

So that we might learn conclusively and in detail about the fate of the human transports leaving the Ghetto, Zalmen Frydrych (Zygmunt) was ordered to follow one of the transports to the 'Aryan side'. His journey 'to the East', however, was a short one, for it took only three days. Immediately after leaving the Ghetto walls he established contact with an employee of the Warsaw Danzig Terminal working on the Warsaw-Malkinia line. They travelled together in the transport's wake to Sokolow where, Zygmunt was told by local railroad men, the tracks forked out, one branch leading to Treblinka. It developed that every day a freight train carrying people from Warsaw travelled in that direction and invariably returned empty. No transports of food were ever seen on this line. Civilians were forbidden to approach the Treblinka railroad station.

This in itself was conclusive proof that the people brought to Treblinka were being exterminated somewhere in the vicinity. In addition, Zygmunt met two fugitives from the death camp the following morning. They were two Jews, completely stripped of their clothes, and Zygmunt met them on the Sokolow market place and obtained the full details of the horrible procedure. Thus it was not any longer a question of rumours, but of facts established by eye-witness accounts (one of the fugitives was comrade Wallach).

After Zygmunt's return we published the second issue of **On Guard** with a detailed description of Treblinka. But even now the population stubbornly refused to believe the truth. They simply closed their eyes to the unpleasant facts and fought against them with all the means at their disposal.

In the meantime the Germans, not too discriminative in their choice of methods, introduced a new propaganda twist. They promised—and actually gave—three kilograms of bread and one kilogram of marmalade to everyone who voluntarily registered for 'deportation'. The offer was more than sufficient. Once the bait was thrown, propaganda and hunger did the rest. The propaganda value of the measure lay in the fact that it was truly an excellent argument against the 'stories' about gas-chambers ('why would they be giving bread away if they intended to murder them?...'). The hunger, an even stronger persuader, magnified the picture of three brown, crusty loaves of bread until nothing was visible beyond it. Their taste which one could almost feel in one's mouth—it was only a short walk from one's home to the *Umschlagplatz* from which the cars left —blinded people to all the other things at the end of the same road. Their smell, familiar, delicious, befogged one's mind, made it unable to grasp the things which would normally have been so very obvious. There were times when hundreds of people had to wait in line for several days to be 'deported'. The number of people anxious to obtain the three kilograms of bread was such that the transports, now leaving twice daily with 12,000 people, could not accommodate them all.

The noose around the Ghetto was now becoming tighter and tighter. After a short period of time all of the so-called 'Little Ghetto' (the neighbourhood of Twarda and Panska Streets) had been emptied of all its inhabitants. In ten days all 'volunteers', children's homes ('Korczak's Children'), and refugee shelters were shipped out, and the systematic 'blockades' of city blocks and streets began. People with knapsacks would escape from street to street, trying to guess in advance the area of the next 'blockade', and stay away from it.

* * *

The gendarmes, Ukrainians and Jewish Police cooperate nicely. The roles are meticulously and precisely divided. The gendarmes surround the streets; the Ukrainians, in front of the gendarmes, encircle the houses closely; the Jewish Police walk into the courtyards and summon all the inhabitants. 'All Jews must come down. Thirty kilograms of baggage allowed. Those remaining inside shall be shot...' And once again, the same summons. People run from all staircases. Nervously, on the run, they clothe themselves in whatever is handy. Some descend as they are, sometimes straight from bed, others are carrying everything they can possibly take along, knapsacks, packages, pots and pans. People cast frightened glances at one another, the worst has happened. Trembling, they form groups in front of the house. They are not allowed to talk but they still try to gain the policemen's pity. From nearby houses similar groups of trembling, completely exasperated people arrive and form into one long column. A gendarme beckons with his rifle to a casual passer-by who, having been warned too late, was unable to escape the doomed street. A Jewish policeman pulls him by his sleeve or by his neck into the column in front of the house. If the policeman is halfway decent, he hides a small piece of paper with the scribbled address of the victim's family—to let them know... Now the deserted houses, the apartment entrances ajar according to regulations, are given a quick once-over by the Ukrainians. They open closed apartments with a single kick of their heavy boots, with a single blow of a rifle butt. Two, three shots signify the death of those people who did not heed the call and remained in their homes. The 'blockade' is finished. On somebody's table an unfinished cup of tea gets cold, flies finish somebody's piece of bread.

People outside of the 'blockaded' area hopelessly look for relatives and friends among the rectangular groups surrounded by Ukrainians and Jewish policemen. The columns slowly march through the streets. Behind them, in a single row, requisitioned 'rickshaws' carry the old and the children.

It is a long way to the *Umschlag*. The Deportation Point, from which the cars leave, is situated on the very edge of the Ghetto, on Stawki Street. The tall walls surrounding it and closely guarded by gendarmes are broken at only one narrow place. Through this entrance the groups of helpless powerless people are brought in. Everyone holds some papers, working certificates, identification cards. The gendarme at the entrance looks them over briefly. 'Rechts'—means life; 'links'—means death. Although everyone knows in advance the futility of all arguments, he still tries to show his particular helpfulness to German industry, to his particular German master, and thus hopes to receive the magic little order, 'rechts'. The gendarme does not even listen. Sometimes he orders the passing people to show their hands—he chooses all small ones: 'rechts'; sometimes he separates blondes: 'links'; in the morning he favours short people; in the evening he takes a liking to tall ones. 'Links', 'links', 'links'.

The human torrent grows, deepens, floods three large three-storey buildings, former schools. More people are assembled here than are necessary to fill the next four days' quota, they are just being brought in as 'reserves'. People wait four or five days before they are loaded into the railroad cars. People fill every inch of free space, crowd the buildings, bivouac in empty rooms, hallways, on the stairs. Dirty, slimy mud floods the floors. One's foot sinks in human excrements at every step. The odour of sweat and urine sticks in one's throat. There are no panes in the windows, and the nights are cold. Some are dressed only in nightshirts or housecoats.

On the second day hunger begins to twist the stomach in painful spasms, cracked lips long for a drop of water. The times when people were given three loaves of bread are long since gone. Sweating, feverish children lie helplessly in their mothers' arms. People seem to shrink, become smaller, greyer.

All eyes have a wild, crazy, fearful look. People look pale, helpless, desperate. There is a sudden flash of revelation that soon the worst, the incredible, the thing one would not believe to the very last moment is bound to happen. Here, in this crowded square, all the continually nursed illusions collapse, all the brittle hopes that 'Maybe I may save myself and my dearest ones from total destruction'...collapse. A nightmare settles on one's chest, grips one's throat, shoves one's eyes out of their sockets, opens one's mouth to a soundless cry. An old man imploringly and feverishly hangs on to strangers around him. A helplessly suffering mother presses three children to her heart. One wants to yell, but there is nobody to yell to; to implore, to argue—there is nobody to argue with; one is alone, completely alone in this multitudinous crowd. One can almost feel the ten—nay, hundred, thousand—rifles aimed at one's heart. The figures of the Ukrainians grow to gigantic proportions. And then one does not know of anything any more, does not think about anything , one sits down dully in a corner, right in the mud and fung of the wet floor. The air becomes more and more stuffy, the place becomes mcre and more crowded, not because of the thousands of bodies and the odour of the rooms, but because of the sudden understanding that all is lost, that nothing can be done, that one must perish.

Possibilities of leaving the *Umschlag* did exist, but they were a drop in the sea of the thousands awaiting help. The Germans themselves established these possibilities when they transferred a small children's hospital from the Little Ghetto into one of the *Umschlag* buildings and opened an emergency aid station there—a malicious gesture toward those sentenced to death. Twice daily, in the morning and the evening, the personnel working in the aid station was changed. All the aid station workers were clad in white coats and all were issued working certificates. Thus it was sufficient to dress somebody in a white coat to enable him to be taken out with the crew of doctors and nurses. Some nurses took strange children into their arms and walked out with them claiming they were their own. With older people the matter was more difficult. These could only be sent 'to the cemetery' or to a hospital for adults situated outside the enclosure, a procedure likewise sanctioned by the Germans for no apparent reason. Thus, healthy people were smuggled out of the '*Umschlag* ground' in ambulances and in coffins. After a while, however, the Germans began to check the ambulances and the condition of the 'sick'. Therefore, in order to show undeniable evidence, those old men and women whose death was slated to be temporarily postponed, by virtue of somebody's intervention or as a personal favour, were brought to a small room in the aid station, behind the reception room. Here their legs were broken without anaesthesia.

In addition, the Jewish Police also 'helped', charging incredible amounts of money, gold or valuables per 'head' for a chance to escape. Those who were rescued, however, a comparatively insignificant number, usually showed up at the *Umschlag* for a second and third time, and finally disappeared into the fatal interior of a railroad car with the rest of the victims.

But people made fanatic efforts to get out of the doomed place. They would cling to the coats of passing nurses begging for a white coat and storm the doors of the hospital guarded by Jewish policemen.

* * *

A father asks that at least his child be admitted. Dr Anna Braude-Heller, Head of the Bersons and Baumans Hospital, takes it from his arms and forcibly pushes it past the protesting guard, into the hospital.

Helena Szefner, pale and beside herself, brought to the *Umschlag* after the last blockade, is also taken into the hospital by our comrades and is then, at the first opportunity, taken outside the walls on a doctor's certificate.

Janek Stroz is stopped by a Jewish policeman as he is about to be led out of the enclosure. It looks as if he is lost, but we terrorise the policeman just behind the gendarme's back and he lets Janek through.

* * *

It often happened that the messenger sent to help somebody escape from the *Umschlag* was not only unable to complete his mission, but perished himself, swept with the crowd into a railroad car. Samek Kostrynski, one of our bravest sent to the *Umschlag* for some of our comrades, met death in such a manner.

The most important and most difficult thing in the *Umschlag* was to live through the time when the cars were being loaded. The transports left in the mornings and evenings. The loading took place twice daily. An endless chain of Ukrainians would encircle the square and the thousandfold crowd. Shots would be fired and every shot hit its target. It was not difficult to hit when one had within a few paces a thick, moving crowd, every particle of which was a living person, a target. The shots drew the crowd nearer and nearer to the waiting cattle cars. Not enough! Like mad beasts the Ukrainians ran through the empty square toward the buildings. Here a wild chase would begin. The frightened crowd hurried to the upper floors, gathered in front of the hospital doors, hid in dark holes in the attic. Just to get away, higher up, further from the chase. One might be lucky enough to miss one more transport, save another day of life. Comrade Mendelson (Mendele) remained in an attic for three days. A few girls, Skif members, hid there for five days and were later led out with a group of nurses.

The Ukrainians did not exert themselves unnecessarily. The number of those who could not escape fast enough was always sufficient to fill the cars. The last moment before the departure, a mother is pushed into a car, but there is no more room for her child, which is pulled away from her and loaded further down the line, in the next incomplete car. Resistance? An instant shot. Slowly, with difficulty, the doors close. The crowd is so thick that it has to be mashed in with the rifle butts. And then, the train starts. Fresh fodder for the Treblinka gas-chambers is under way.

During this time we lost almost all of our comrades. Just a few dozen of our members remained from our original group numbering more than 500 people. The Hechalutz Organisation had better luck. It remained almost intact. They started a few fires for diversionary purposes and carried out an assault on the Jewish Police commander, J Szerynski.

The best from among us were deported in such a manner in the beginning of August, 1942. S Kostrynski, I Szpilberg, Pola Lipszyc, Cywia Waks, Mania Elenbogen, Kuba Zylberberg, all were sent out. Hanusia Wasser and her mother Mania Wasser perished, as did Halinka Brandes and her mother. Comrade Orzech, sought by the Gestapo on several occasions, had to flee to the 'Aryan side'.

On 13 August, 1942, Sonia Nowogrodzka was taken from the W C Toebbens factory. It was strange. Only two days previously Sonia, looking out of the window at the crowd returning from work, had said: 'My place is not here. Look who remains in the Ghetto, only the scum. The working masses march in formation to the *Umschlag*. I have to go with them. If I shall be with them, then, perhaps, they will not forget that they are human beings even during their last moments, in the cars, and afterwards...'

A small handful of us remained. We did all we could, but only very little *was* possible. We wanted to save whatever we could at any price. We placed our people in German establishments, the very best it seemed. Just the same we began losing contact with one another. Only one larger group of comrades was able to keep together (20-25 people), the one at the 'brushmakers' shops' at Franciszkanska Street.

This was our most tragic period. We could plainly see the slow disappearance of our whole organisation. We could see that everything we had so carefully nursed through the long and difficult years of war was crumbling, part of the general desolation, that all our work and efforts were of no avail. It was mostly due to Abrasha Blum, to his composure and presence of mind, that we weathered the nightmare of those terrible times.

At about the middle of September, when only 120,000 people were left in the Ghetto, the first part of the 'action' appeared to have ended. The *Umsiedlungsstab* left Warsaw then without any instructions as to the future. But even now hopes proved futile. It quickly became clear that the Germans were using the short pause to liquidate Jewish settlements in nearby towns—Otwock, Falenica, Miedzeszyn. The entire staff and all the children of the W Medem Sanitarium were deported from Miedzeszyn. Roza Eichner died a martyr's death

After this temporary let-up, the deportations from Warsaw started again with intensified force. Now the blockades were even more dangerous for us, because there were fewer people and the area had become smaller. They were also more difficult for the Germans, however, because people had already learned how to hide. Therefore, a new method was used: every Jewish policeman was made responsible for bringing seven 'heads' daily to the 'Umschlag.' So that they would furnish the required seven 'heads', Jewish policemen would stop a doctor in a white coat (the coat could be sold for a fantastically high price later, in the *Umschlag*...), a mother with her child in her arms, or a lonely, lost child in search of its home.

Yes, the Jewish Police certainly wrote their own history by their deeds.

On 6 September, 1942, all remaining Ghetto inhabitants were ordered to report to an area bounded by the following streets: Gesia, Zamenhofa, Lubeckiego, Stawki. Here the final registration was to take place.

* * *

From all directions people march, four abreast, to the designated spot. All our friends are here, too. We hear Ruta Perenson tell her little Nick: 'You must not be afraid of anything. Terrible things are going to happen soon. They want to kill us all, but we shan't let them. We shall hit them just as badly as they will hit us...'

* * *

This, however, did not happen. The entire Ghetto population was assembled in the small rectangle of the designated block: the workers of the plants, the Jewish Council employees, the public health workers, the hospital workers (the sick were sent directly to the *Umschlag*). The Germans named a limited number of people who were permitted to remain in every German establishment, and in the Jewish Council. Those chosen individuals received numbered slips of paper, a guarantee of life. The chances of receiving such a life-insuring paper were almost nil, but the mere fact that such chances did exist was sufficient to confuse people, to cause their attention to converge solely on the means of securing a numbered slip. Everything else was suddenly of no importance. Some fought for the piece of paper loudly, shrilly attempting to prove their right to live. Others, tearfully resigned, meekly awaited their fate. The last selection took place in a state of utmost tension. After two days, every hour of which seemed to last ages, the chosen ones were escorted back to their places of work, where they were henceforth to be billeted. The remainder was led to the *Umschlag*. The last to arrive here were the families of the Jewish policemen.

* * *

No words of any human language are strong enough to describe the *Umschlag* now, when no help from anywhere or anybody can be expected. The sick, adults as well as children, previously brought here from the hospital, lie deserted in the cold halls. They relieve themselves right where they lie, and remain in the stinking slime of excrements and urine. Nurses search the crowd for their fathers and mothers and, having found them, inject longed-for deathly morphine into their veins, their own eyes gleaming wildly. One doctor compassionately pours a cyanide solution into the feverish mouths of strange, sick children. To offer one's cyanide to somebody else is now the most precious, the most irreplaceable thing. It brings a quiet, peaceful death, it saves from the horror of the cars.

* * *

Thus the Germans deported 60,000 people within two days.

From the 'Kettle' the following of our comrades were deported: Natan Liebeskind, Dora Kociolek, J. Gruszka, Anka Wolkowicz, Michelson, Cluwa Krysztal-Nisenbaum, and many others. Comrade Bernard Goldsztejn, for whom the Germans were specifically searching, had to hide on the 'Aryan side'.

On 12 September the 'action' was officially ended. A nominal number of 33,400 Jews working in factories and for German employers, 3000 employees of the Jewish Council included, remained in Warsaw. Actually, counting the people who had been able to remain hidden in cellars and other such places, the number of remaining Jews was approximately 60,000. All were billeted at their working posts. New walls divided the ghetto, and between the inhabited blocks there were vast, empty, desolated areas, haunted by the dead quiet of the street, the tapping of the open window frames in the wind, and the sickly stench of unburied corpses.

By now the Ghetto comprised: (1) The area of Toebben's, Schultz's, Roehrich's shops—Leszno Street, Karmelicka Street, Nowolipki Street, Smocza, Nowolipie and Zelazna Street up to Leszno; (2) The 'brushmakers' area'—Sto Jerska Street, Walowa, Franciszkanska, and Bonifraterska Street up to Sto Jerska; (3) The 'Central Ghetto'—Gesia Street, Franciszkanska, Bonifraterska, Muranowska, Pokorna, Stawki, Parysowski Square, and Smocza Street up to Gesia.

Workers of one shop were now forbidden to communicate with those of another. The Germans exploited to the utmost the lives of those whom they had spared. The usual working hours for Jews were twelve hours daily, and sometimes even longer, without interruption, while the working and the food conditions were simply catastrophic. As in the first period, when spotted fever conditions had been the Ghetto's plague, epidemics again ravaged the Ghetto. This time tuberculosis was rampant. Only the garbage collectors and the gravediggers (the so-called 'Pinkert-Boys'—a name derived from the name of a well-known Jewish Funeral home) became wealthy, transporting to the 'Aryan side' in coffins and under garbage piles valuables which the Ghetto could no longer use. It became the dream of every inhabitant of the harassed Jewish section to escape to the 'Aryan side' and to establish himself there.

In the beginning of October, 1942, talks between our own Executive Committee and the Command of the Hechalutz Battle Organisation took place. The purpose of the talks was the establishment of a joint organisation. This matter, argued back and forth among our comrades , was finally settled at a meeting of the Warsaw Party cadres which took place on 15 October. We then decided that a joint battle organisation should be formed, and that its purpose should be to prepare armed resistance for the time when the Germans might attempt to repeat the extermination procedure in the Warsaw Ghetto. We realised that only through coordinated work and our utmost joint efforts could any results at all be expected.

About 20 October the so-called Coordinating Committee (KK), whose members were representatives of all existing political parties, was formed. Abrasha Blum and Berek Sznajdmil represented us on the KK. At the same time the Command of the new Jewish Battle Organisation (ZOB) was appointed. Morchaj Anilewicz ('Hashomer') became the ZOB's Commander. Marek Edelman was called into the Command to represent our groups. Dr I Fajner ('Mikolaj') undertook to represent the KK on the 'Aryan side', on our behalf. An executive committee for the KK was also appointed, as was a propaganda committee. Abrasha Blum represented us on these committees.

Since the Ghetto was divided into separate areas between which there was almost no contact, the ZOB necessarily had to organise its work accordingly. We took over the leadership in the 'brushmaker's region' (Grylak), the W C Toebbens area (Paw), and the Prosta Street neighbourhood (Kersz). We succeeded in forming several battle groups. Thus B Pelc and Goldsztejn led two 'fives' in the Central Ghetto; Jurek Blones and Janek Bilak headed two 'fives' in the 'brushmakers' region'; A Fajner and N Chmielnicki were the leaders in the Schultz area; W Rozowski led our group at the Roehrich shop.

Once again we built a large organisation, not alone this time, but by common efforts, and once again a major problem of weapons was encountered. There were almost none at all in the Ghetto. It must be taken into account that the time was the year 1942. The resistance movement of the Poles was just beginning at the time, and only vague stories were being circulated about partisans in the woods. It must be remembered that the first organised act of armed resistance on the part of the Poles did not take place until March, 1943. Therefore, there was nothing unusual in the fact that our efforts to obtain arms and ammunition through the Government Delegate and through other agencies encountered major difficulties and, as a general rule, brought no results. We were able to obtain a few pistols from the People's Guard. Afterwards two assaults took place: on the Commander of the Jewish Police, Lejkin, on 29 October; and on J First (the Jewish Council's representative at the *Umsiedlungsstab*) on 29 November.

And so the ZOB gained its first popularity. It carried out several more assaults against a few Jewish foremen who caused most of the suffering on the part of the Jewish slave-labourers. During such an assault in the Hallman area (Hallman's was a cabinet maker's shop), German factory guards arrested three of the participants. At night, however, our group from the Roehrich area, led by G Fryszdorf, disarmed the German guards and freed our prisoners.

The following incident may serve to clarify the conditions in which we had to work at the time. About mid-November (in the period of 'quiet') a few hundred Jews from several shops were deported, allegedly to work in the Lublin Concentration Camp. During the trip Comrade W Rozowski broke open the bars in the car window, threw out six female prisoners while the train was in motion (among others, Guta Blones, Chajka Belchatowska, Wiernik, M Kojfman), and then jumped out himself. Similar feats would have been quite impossible to perform at the time of the first deportations, because even if there had been somebody brave enough to attempt an escape, the other victims would never have allowed it for fear of German revenge. By now the Jews finally began to realise that deportation actually meant death; that there was no other alternative but at least to die honourably. But as was quite natural for human beings, they still tried to postpone death and 'honour' for as long a time as possible.

At the end of December, 1942, we received our first transport of weapons from the Home Army. It wasn't much —there were only ten pistols in the whole transport—but it enabled us to prepare for our first major action. We planned it for 22 January, and it was to be a retaliatory measure against the Jewish Police.

However, on 18 January, 1943, the Ghetto was surrounded once again and the 'second liquidation' began. This time, however, the Germans were not able to carry out their plans unchallenged. Four barricaded battle groups offered the first armed resistance in the Ghetto.

The ZOB was baptised in battle in the first large-scale street fighting at the corner of Mila and Zamenhofa Streets. The best part of the organisation was lost there. Miraculously, because of his heroic attitude, the ZOB Commander, Mordchaj Anilewicz, survived. After that battle we realised that street fighting would be too costly for us, since we were not sufficiently prepared for it and lacked proper weapons. We, therefore, switched to partisan fighting. Four major encounters were fought in the apartment houses at 40 Zamenhofa Street, 44 Muranowska Street, 34 Mila Street and 22 Franciszkanska Street. In the Schultz Shop area the SS men taking part in the deportation were attacked by the partisans. Comrade A Fajner took an active part in this action and was killed in its course.

One of our battle groups, still unarmed, was caught by the Germans and was taken to the *Umschlag*. Shortly before they were to enter the railroad cars, B Pelc addressed the group with a few words. It was only a short address, but it was so effective that not a single one of the sixty people moved to enter the car. Van Oeppen (the chief of Treblinka) shot all sixty himself on the spot. This group's behaviour, however, served as an inspiration that always, under all circumstances, one should oppose the Germans.

Of all the prepared battle groups only five took part in the January activities. The remainder, not having been assembled at the time of the Germans' entry into the Ghetto, was caught by surprise and was unable to reach the place where their weapons were stored.

Once again, as was the case in the first stage of the ZOB's activities, four-fifths of the Battle Organisation's members perished.

The latest developments, however, reverberated strongly

both within the Ghetto and outside of it. Public opinion, Jewish as well as Polish, reacted immediately to the Ghetto battles. For now, for the first time, German plans were frustrated. For the first time the halo of omnipotence and invincibility was torn from the Germans' heads. For the first time the Jew in the street realised that it *was* possible to do something against the Germans' will and power. The number of Germans killed by ZOB bullets was not the only important thing. What was more important was the appearance of a psychological turning point. The mere fact that because of the unexpected resistance, weak as it was, the Germans were forced to interrupt their 'deportation' schedule was of great value.

In the meantime legends about 'hundreds' of dead Germans and the 'tremendous' power of the ZOB started circulating throughout Warsaw. The entire Polish Underground was full of praise for us. At the end of January we received 50 larger pistols and 55 hand grenades from the Home Army Command. A reorganisation of the ZOB was carried out. All battle groups were now divided among four major areas. We commanded the 'brushmakers' area' (Marek Edelman was in command), where we had , among others, our own battle group led by Jurek Blones. The battle groups were quartered in the immediate vicinity of their operational posts. The purpose of the billeting arrangement was to prevent groups from being taken by surprise by new German regulations, as had happened before, and to accustom the partisans to military discipline, military ways, and a continual use of their weapons. In the vicinity of the Ghetto walls we established guard posts and guards, instructed to inform immediately about approaching danger, kept vigil 24 hours a day.

In the meantime the German propaganda machine worked and tried once more to distract the Jews with invented stories about 'Jewish reservations in Trawniki and Poniatow' where the Toebbens and Schultz factories were allegedly to be evacuated and where 'productive Jews devotedly working for the Germans would be able to live through the war in peace'. In the beginning of February, 1943, the Germans brought into the Ghetto twelve Jewish foremen from the Lublin Concentration Camp who were to persuade the Ghetto population to volunteer for work 'under excellent conditions'. The night following the arrival of these individuals ZOB members encircled their quarters and forced their immediate departure from the Ghetto. But the Germans tried once more. They nominated W C Toebbens, the proprietor of the largest Ghetto factory, manufacturing German uniforms, to the post of Deportation Commissar. This move was designed to create further impressions that the 'evacuation to Trawniki and Poniatow' was closely related to the need for workers in German enterprises.

The ZOB also conducted large-scale propaganda activities. Several proclamations were published and posted on the Ghetto walls and houses. In reply, Toebbens prepared his own appeal to the Jewish population both editions of which, however, were confiscated in the printing shop by the ZOB.

During this period the ZOB alone ruled the Ghetto. It was the only force and the only authority recognised by public opinion.

When, at the end of January, 1943, the Germans appealed to the workers to evacuate Hallman's cabinetmakers' shop, of the more than 1000 workers employed only twenty-five heeded the call. At night, in a daring patrol, two battle groups set the shop's stores afire (Comrade Fryszdorf took part in this action), causing losses of more than a million *zloty* to the Germans. Once again well-laid German plans were upset. The following morning the Germans issued a communiqué blaming the fire on parachutists. Nonetheless, the Jewish population knew perfectly well who had actually been behind the fire and who had really caused the Germans to lose face.

At the beginning of March the Germans again appealed to the Brushmakers' Shop to register for evacuation, but not a single one of the 3500 workers registered. The ZOB, on the other hand, carried out its plans to the last detail: the transport of brushmaking machinery, loaded on to railway cars on the *Umschlagplatz*, burned up on its way, due to our planting of special incendiary bottles with delayed-action fuses.

The Germans became more and more uncomfortable in the Ghetto. They became increasingly aware of the hostile attitude not only of the battle groups, but also of the population as a whole, which willingly carried out all ZOB instructions.

The ZOB broadened its activities and was supported by the whole Ghetto. Bakers and merchants delivered quantities of food for its members. The wealthy inhabitants were taxed by it, and the funds thus secured were used for the purchase of arms and ammunition. The ZOB determined the amount of contributions to be paid by the Jewish Community agencies. The discipline was such that everybody had to pay either voluntarily or forcibly. The Jewish Council contributed 250,000 *zloty*. The Office for Economic Requirements (*Zaklad Zaopatrywania*) paid 710,000 *zloty*. Revenues over the period of the first three months amounted to about ten million *zloty*. These sums were smuggled over to the 'Aryan side' where our representatives organised the purchase of weapons and explosives.

Arms were smuggled into the Ghetto in precisely the same manner as other contraband. Bribed Polish policemen closed their eyes to heavy parcels thrown over the Ghetto walls at designated spots. ZOB liaison men immediately disposed of the packages. The Jewish policemen guarding the Ghetto walls had no voice in the matter. Our most active liaison men with the 'Aryan side' were Zygmunt Frydrych (who arranged the first transport of weapons), Michal Klepfisz, Celemenski, Fajgele Peltel (Wladka), and many others. Michal Klepfisz, in cooperation with the PS and WRN groups,[15] made the necessary arrangements for a large-scale purchase of explosives and incendiaries (for example 2000 litres of gasoline) and later, after transporting the shipment to the Ghetto, set up a factory for the production of Molotov cocktails and hand grenades. The production process was primitive and simple, but the large output of the shop increased the firing power of our detachments. By now every partisan was equipped, on the average, with one pistol (and ten to fifteen rounds for it), four or five hand grenades, four or five Molotov cocktails. Two or three rifles were assigned to each 'area'.

There was just one machine gun in the entire Ghetto.

The ZOB now carried out a programme designed to rid the Jewish population of hostile elements and of those individuals who collaborated with the Germans. It carried out death sentences pronounced by its Command on almost all Jewish Gestapo agents. Those whom our justice did not reach were forced to steal away to the 'Aryan side' and did not dare return to the Ghetto. Once, when four Gestapo members appeared unexpectedly in the Ghetto for half an hour, three were killed and the fourth was heavily wounded. The notorious Gestapo agent, Dr Alfred Nossig, was also killed, and a Gestapo identification card issued as far back as 1933 was found on his person.

During a meeting of the ZOB Command in the first days of April we resolved to extend our activities to include the entire area of the General Government. A special committee was appointed. At the same time the Bund Central Committee also appointed a committee comprising M Orzech, Dr L Fajner, Bernard Goldsztejn, S Fiszgrund, Celemenski, Samsonowicz to operate on the 'Aryan side.'

The Germans apparently came to the conclusion that the remaining Jews could not be persuaded to leave the Warsaw Ghetto voluntarily. 'Nabbing patrols' were, therefore, organised once again to operate in the Ghetto. At the same time German factory guards jailed several dozen Jews, arrested on the Ghetto streets for minor violations and destined to be evacuated to the Poniatow Camp the following morning. The ZOB Command, however, decided otherwise. At 5.30pm armed ZOB men appeared in the guardhouse where the victims were being held, terrorised the policemen and freed the arrested Jews. The German detachment on guard next door was afraid to intervene.

The Germans, therefore, tried still another method. People arrested in the streets were now immediately loaded on trucks and directed to the *Umschlag*. But the ZOB was still faster: the victims were freed in the areas between the particular blocks (in the so-called 'inter-Ghetto'), where ZOB battle groups were deployed.

In the period immediately preceding the final extermination drive the Bund maintained four barracked battle groups: (1) in the brushmakers' area, led by Jurek Blones; (2) in the Schultz factories area, under the leadership of W Rozowski; (3) two groups in the Central Ghetto area, led by L Gruzalc and Dawid Hochberg, respectively.

Finally, the Germans decided to liquidate the Warsaw Ghetto completely, regardless of cost. On 19 April, 1943, at 2am, the first messages concerning the Germans' approach arrived from our outermost observation posts. These reports made it clear that German gendarmes, aided by Polish 'navy-blue' policemen, were encircling the outer Ghetto walls at 30-yard intervals. An emergency alarm to all our battle groups was immediately ordered, and at 2.15am, that is 15 minutes later, all the groups were already at their battle stations. We also informed the entire population of the imminent danger, and most of the Ghetto inhabitants moved instantly to previously prepared shelters and hide-outs in the cellars and attics of buildings. A deathly silence enveloped the Ghetto. The ZOB was on the alert.

At 4am the Germans, in groups of threes, fours, or fives, so as not to arouse the ZOB's or the population's suspicion, began penetrating into the 'inter-Ghetto' areas. Here they formed into platoons and companies. At seven o'clock motorised detachments, including a number of tanks and armoured vehicles, entered the Ghetto. Artillery pieces were placed outside the walls. Now the SS men were ready to attack. In closed formations, stepping haughtily and loudly, they marched into the seemingly dead streets of the Central Ghetto. Their triumph appeared to be complete. It looked as if this superbly equipped modern army had scared off the handful of bravado-drunk men, as if those few immature boys had at last realised that there was no point in attempting the unfeasible, that they understood that the Germans had more rifles than there were rounds for all their pistols.

But no, they did not scare us and we were not taken by surprise. We were only awaiting an opportune moment. Such a moment presently arrived. The Germans chose the intersection at Mila and Zamenhofa Streets for their bivouac area, and battle groups barricaded at the four corners of the street opened concentric fire on them. Strange projectiles began exploding everywhere (the hand grenades of our own make), the lone machine pistol sent shots through the air now and then (ammunition had to be conserved carefully), rifles started firing a bit further away. Such was the beginning.

The Germans attempted a retreat, but their path was cut. German dead soon littered the street. The remainder tried to find cover in the neighbouring stores and house entrances, but this shelter proved insufficient. The 'glorious' SS, therefore, called tanks into action under the cover of which the remaining men of two companies were to commence a 'victorious' retreat. But even the tanks seemed to be affected by the Germans' bad luck. The first was burned out by one of our incendiary bottles, the rest did not approach our positions. The fate of the Germans caught in the Mila Street-Zamenhofa Street trap was settled. Not a single German left this area alive. The following battle groups took part in the fighting here: Gruzalc's Bund; Merdek's (Hashomer); Hochberg's (Bund); Berek's (Dror); Pawel's (PPR).[16]

Simultaneously, fights were going on at the intersection of Nalewki and Gesia Streets. Two battle groups kept the Germans from entering the Ghetto area at this point. The fighting lasted more than seven hours. The Germans found some mattresses and used them as cover, but the partisans' well- aimed fire forced them to several successive withdrawals. German blood flooded the street. German ambulances continuously transported their wounded to the small square near the Community buildings. Here the wounded lay in rows on the sidewalk awaiting their turn to be admitted to the hospital. At the corner of Gesia Street a German air liaison observation post signalled the partisans' positions and the required bombing targets to the planes. But from the air as well as on the ground the partisans appeared to be invincible. The Gesia Street-Nalewki Street battle ended in the complete withdrawal of the Germans.

At the same time heavy fighting raged at Muranowski

Square. Here the Germans attacked from all directions. The cornered partisans defended themselves bitterly and succeeded, by truly superhuman efforts, in repulsing the attacks. Two German machine guns as well as a quantity of other weapons were captured. A German tank was burned, the second tank of the day.

At 2pm, not a single live German remained in the Ghetto area. It was the ZOB's first complete victory over the Germans. The remaining hours of the day passed in 'complete quiet', that is with the exception of artillery fire (the guns were in positions at Krasinskich Square) and several bombings from the air.

The following day there was silence until 2pm. At that time the Germans, again in closed formation, arrived at the brushmakers' gate. They did not suspect that at that very moment an observer lifted an electric plug. A German factory guard walked toward the gate wanting to open it. At precisely the same moment the plug was placed in the socket and a mine, waiting for the Germans for a long time, exploded under the SS men's feet. Over one hundred SS men were killed in the explosion. The rest, fired on by the partisans, withdrew.

Two hours later the Germans tried their luck once again. In a different manner now, carefully, one after another, in extended order formations, they attempted to penetrate into the brushmakers' area. Here, however, they were again suitably received by a battle group awaiting them. Of the thirty Germans who succeeded in entering the area, only a few were able to leave it. Once again the Germans withdrew from the Ghetto. Once again the partisans' victory was complete. It was their second victory.

The Germans tried again. They attempted to enter the Ghetto at several other points, and everywhere they encountered determined opposition. Every house was a fortress.

* * *

In one of the attics we are suddenly surrounded.
Nearby, in the same attic, are the Germans and it is
impossible to reach the stairs. In the dark corners of the attic

we cannot even see one another. We do not notice Sewek Dunski and Junghajzer who crawl up the stairs from below, reach the attic, get behind the Germans and throw a grenade. We do not even pause to consider how it happens that Michal Klepfisz jumps straight on to the German machine pistol firing from behind the chimney. We only see the cleared path. After the Germans have been thrown out, several hours later, we find Michal's body perforated like a sieve from two machine pistol series.

*   *   *

The brushmakers' area could not be taken

Now something unprecedented took place. Three officers with lowered machine pistols appeared. They wore white rosettes in their buttonholes—emissaries. They desired to negotiate with the Area Command. They proposed a 15-minute truce to remove the dead and the wounded. They were also ready to promise all inhabitants an orderly evacuation to working camps in Poniatow and Trawniki, and to let them take along all their belongings.

Firing was our answer. Every house remained a hostile fortress. From every storey, from every window bullets sought hated German helmets, hated German hearts.

*   *   *

On the fourth storey, at a small window, our soldier Diament is at his combat post. His is a long rifle whose glorious history reaches back to the Russo-Japanese War. Diament is phlegmatic, his movements are slow but deliberate. The young boys near him impatiently try to hurry him along. But Diament is imperturbable. He aims at the stomach, hits the heart. Every round finishes off another German.

At the second-storey window is Dwojra, firing away rancorously. The Germans spot her: *'Schau, Hans, eine Frau schiesst!'* They try to get her, but somehow their bullets miss. She, apparently, does not miss often, for, strangely enough, they withdraw quickly.

On the first floor, on the stairway (Post No. 1), are Szlamek Szuster and Kazik throwing one hand grenade after another. After a while the supply of grenades becomes exhausted, while two Germans are still moving about the courtyard below. Szlamek reaches for an incendiary bottle and throws it at the German so accurately that the later, hit squarely over his helmet, instantly catches fire and is burned to death.

*   *   *

The partisans' stand was so determined that the Germans were finally forced to abandon all ordinary fighting methods and to try new, apparently infallible tactics. Their new idea was to set fire to the entire brushmakers' block from the outside, on all sides simultaneously. In an instant fires were raging over the entire block, black smoke choked one's throat, burned one's eyes. The partisans, naturally, did not intend to be burnt alive in the flames. We decided to gamble for our lives and attempt to reach the Central Ghetto area regardless of consequences.

*   *   *

The flames cling to our clothes, which now start smouldering. The pavement melts under our feet into a black, gooey substance. Broken glass, littering every inch of the streets, is transformed into a sticky liquid in which our feet are caught. Our soles begin to burn from the heat of the stone pavement. One after another we stagger through the conflagration. From house to house, from courtyard to courtyard, with no air to breathe, with a hundred hammers clanging in our heads, with burning rafters continuously falling over us, we finally reach the end of the area under fire. We feel lucky just to stand here, to be out of the inferno.

Now the most difficult part remains. There is only one possible way into the Central Ghetto—through a small breach in the Wall guarded from three sides by Gendarmes, Ukrainians, and 'navy-blue' police. Five battle groups have to force their way through this breach. One after the other, their feet wrapped in rags to stifle the sound of steps under heavy fire, tense to the utmost, Gutman's, Berlinski's, and Grynbaum's groups force their way through. Success! Jurek Blones' group covers from behind. While the first of this group emerge on the street, a German searchlight illuminates the entire wall section. It seems as if not a single person more will be able to save his life here. Suddenly Romanowicz's single well-aimed round puts out the searchlight and, before the Germans have time to collect their wits, our entire group manages to cross over to the other side.

* * *

We continued the fight in the Central Ghetto in cooperation with the battle groups existing in that area. As in the brushmakers' area before, it was almost impossible to move freely through the area. Entire streets were sometimes blocked by tremendous fires. The sea of flames flooded houses and courtyards, wooden beams burned noisily, walls collapsed. There was no air, only black, choking smoke and heavy, burning heat radiating from the red hot walls, from the glowing stone stairs.

The omnipotent flames were now able to accomplish what the Germans could not do. Thousands of people perished in the conflagration. The stench of burning bodies was everywhere. Charred corpses lay around on balconies, in window recesses, on unburned steps. The flames chased the people out from their shelters, made them leave the previously prepared safe hide-outs in attics and cellars. Thousands staggered about in the courtyards where they were easy prey for the Germans who imprisoned them or killed them outright. Tired beyond all endurance, they would fall asleep in driveways, entrances, standing, sitting, lying and were caught asleep by a passing German's bullet. Nobody would even notice that an old man sleeping in a corner would never again wake up, that a mother feeding her baby had been cold and dead for three days, that a baby's crying and sucking was futile since its mother's arms were cold and her breast dead. Hundreds committed suicide jumping from fourth or fifth stories of apartment houses. Mothers would thus save their children from terrible death in flames. The Polish population saw these scenes from Sto Jerska Street and from Krasinskich Square.

After such exemplary lessons in the Central Ghetto and in the brushmakers' area, the Germans assumed that other shops would no longer oppose a 'voluntary' evacuation from the Ghetto. They, therefore, announced a deadline for appearing at the collection points, threatening with like persecutions in the event of disobedience. By now, however, neither pleading nor threats could convince the population.

The partisans were on the alert everywhere. In the Toebbens and Schultz area they first of all attempted to disrupt the regular movements of German units into the Central Ghetto. From balconies, windows, and rooftops they showered the moving truckloads of SS men with hand grenades and with rifle and pistol fire. Once even a truck speeding on the 'Aryan side' was blown up. On one occasion Rozowski and Szlomo, during the course of an area inspection, noticed an approaching German truck. They thought for an instant, and then swiftly climbed to a balcony. From here they threw a four-pound powder charge straight down into the truck killing all but five of the sixty SS men in it.

After five days the deadline for 'voluntary' evacuation passed and the Germans once again began to 'subdue' the area. They again met with determined opposition. Unfortunately, the previously planted mines could not be set off because by now there was no electric current in the Ghetto. But heavy fighting took place. Partisans, barricaded in the houses, kept the Germans from advancing into the area. As was the case in the other areas, every house fought. Particularly heavy fighting occurred in the following apartment houses: 41 Nowolipki Street, 64 Nowolipie Street, 67 Nowolipie Street, 72 Leszno Street, 56 Leszno Street.

* * *

At 56 Leszno Street Jurek is cornered at an outpost. A group of SS men surrounds him, and one throws a grenade.

Jurek adroitly catches the grenade in mid-air and tosses it back at the SS men before it has time to explode. Four of them are killed on the spot.

Szlomo, the Deputy Area Commander, his arm wounded, covers the withdrawal from 72 Nowolipie Street. Suddenly the group is surrounded. Everything seems lost. There is no time to prevent disaster. Szlomo quickly pulls a sheet from a bed and with it he lowers everyone present down to the courtyard. There is nobody to hold it for him, however, and he jumps from the second storey.

*　*　*

In this area, like in the others, the Germans finally 'saved' their military honour by setting house after house on fire.

In view of the changed conditions, the ZOB now resolved to change its tactics, namely to attempt the protection of larger groups of the population hidden in bunkers and shelters. Thus two ZOB. detachments (Hochberg's and Sznadjmil's) escorted a few hundred people from the ruined shelter at 37 Mila Street to 7 Mila Street in broad daylight. The partisans were able to hold this latter hide-out, where several thousand people found shelter for over a week.

The burning of the Ghetto came to an end. There simply weren't any more living quarters and, still worse, there was no water. The partisans themselves now descended to the underground shelters occupied by the civilian population to defend whatever could still be defended.

Battles and armed encounters were now fought mostly at night, while in the daytime the Ghetto was completely lifeless. The Germans and the ZOB patrols met only when the streets were completely dark, and whoever had time to fire first, won. Our patrols were spread over the entire Ghetto area. A great many died on both sides every night. The Germans and Ukrainians made it a practice to patrol the streets in larger groups, and lay in ambush for the partisans only.

On May Day the Command decided to carry out a 'holiday' action. Several battle groups were sent out to 'hunt down' the greatest number of Germans possible. In the evening, a May

Day roll-call was held. The partisans were briefly addressed by a few people and the 'Internationale' was sung. The entire world, we knew, was celebrating May Day on that day and everywhere forceful, meaningful words were being spoken. But never yet had the 'Internationale' been sung in conditions so different, so tragic, in a place where an entire nation had been and was still perishing. The words and the song echoed from the charred ruins and were, at that particular time, an indication that Socialist youth was still fighting in the Ghetto, and that even in the face of death they were not abandoning their ideals.

The partisans' situation was becoming more grave every hour. Not only were there shortages of food and water, but ammunition was also becoming scarce. We no longer had any communications with the 'Aryan side' and we were, therefore, unable to arrange for the transportation of additional weapons that we had received (on the 'Aryan side') from the People's Army while the fighting in the Ghetto was going on (twenty rifles and ammunition).

The Germans now tried to locate all inhabited shelters by means of sensitive sound-detecting devices and police dogs. On 3 May they located the shelter on 30 Franciszkanska Street, where the operation base of those of our groups who had formerly forced their way from the brushmakers' area was at the time located. Here one of the most brilliant battles was fought. The fighting lasted for two days and half of all our men were killed in its course. A hand grenade killed Berek Sznajdmil. But even in the most difficult moments, when there was almost nothing left, Abrasha Blum kept our spirits up. His presence among us meant more to us and gave us more strength than the possession of the best possible weapon. One can hardly speak of victories when Life itself is the reason for the fight and so many people are lost, but one thing can surely be stated about this particular battle: we did not let the Germans carry out their plans. They did not evacuate a single living person.

On 8 May detachments of Germans and Ukrainians surrounded the Headquarters of the ZOB Command. The fighting lasted two hours, and when the Germans convinced themselves that they would be unable to take the bunker by storm, they tossed in a gas-bomb. Whoever survived the German bullets, whoever was not gassed, committed suicide, for it was quite clear that from here there was no way out, and nobody even considered being taken alive by the Germans. Jurek Wilner called upon all partisans to commit suicide together. Lutek Rotblat shot his mother, his sister, then himself. Ruth fired at herself seven times.

Thus 80 per cent of the remaining partisans perished, among them the ZOB Commander, Mordchaj Anilewicz.

At night the remnants, who had miraculously escaped death, joined the remaining few of the brushmakers' detachments now deployed at 22 Franciszkanska Street.

That very same night two of our liaison men (S Ratajzer —'Kazik', and Franek) arrived from the 'Aryan side'.

Ten days previously the ZOB Command had dispatched Kazik and Zygmunt Frydrych to our representative on the 'Aryan side', Icchak Cukierman ('Antek'), to arrange the withdrawal of the fighting groups through the sewer mains. Now these liaison men arrived.

Unfortunately, it was too late. For one thing, the ZOB was already almost non-existent, but even the remnants that had remained could not all be taken out of the Ghetto together.

All night we walked through the sewers, crawling through numerous entanglements built by the Germans for just such an emergency. The entrance traps were buried under heaps of rubble, the throughways booby-trapped with hand-grenades exploding at a touch. Every once in a while the Germans would let gas into the mains. In similar conditions, in a sewer 28 inches high, where it was impossible to stand up straight and where the water reached our lips, we waited 48 hours for the time to get out. Every minute someone else lost consciousness.

Thirst was the worst handicap. Some even drank the thick slimy sewer water. Every second seemed like months.

On 10 May, at 10am, two trucks halted at the trap door on the Prosta Street-Twarda Street intersection. In broad daylight, with almost no cover whatsoever (the promised

Home Army cover failed and only three of our liaison men and Comrade Krzaczek—a People's Army representative specially detailed for this assignment—patrolled the street), the trap door opened and one after another, with the stunned crowd looking on, armed Jews appeared from the depths of the dark hole (at this time the sight of *any* Jew was already a sensational occurrence. Not all were able to get out. Violently, heavily the trap-door snapped shut, the trucks took off at full speed.

Two battle groups remained in the Ghetto. We were in contact with them until the middle of June. From then on every trace of them disappeared.

Those who had gone over to the 'Aryan side' continued the partisan fight in the woods. The majority perished eventually. The small group that was still alive at the time took an active part in the 1944 Warsaw Uprising as the 'ZOB Group'. At present the following of our comrades are still among the living: Chajka Belchatowska, B Szpigel, Chana Krysztal, Masza Glejtman, and Marek Edelman.

In the period preceding the last German extermination drive the Bund's activities were closely intertwined with the history of the ZOB. I think that never before had there existed a similar degree of unanimity and coordination of people of different political parties as during those various groups' collaboration in that period. We were all fighters for the same just cause, equal in the face of history and death. Every drop of blood was of precisely the same value.

However I should like to mention a few of our comrades, although there were many like them, simply because I came in contact with those particular ones in our daily work.

ABRASHA BLUM. He was the ideological father of armed resistance in our party. Physically very weak, but of exceptional force of conviction and strength of character, he was always the one to decide about our most momentous moves, and he always sided with the youth. He did not permit the flame of zeal and work to die out. Calm and collected in the most difficult moments, he was forever thinking and looking out for somebody else. He simply considered it his duty, as he always did with the most difficult assignment. Whatever he did was simple and obviously the right thing to do. On several occasions friends concerned about his safety urged him to leave the Ghetto and move to the 'Aryan side'. He did not agree to do so, however, wanting to remain in the Ghetto until the very end. And he did remain at his post despite the fact that he was physically unable to fight. He carried no weapons, but he was a partisan nonetheless, at heart. On 3 May, in the course of fighting for the brushmakers' base, when the order 'All to the attack' was given and Abrasha asked the Commander whether it applied to him too, the latter, in the general confusion and without having time to consider, answered 'yes'. Abrasha, unarmed, went to the attack with the others.

JUREK BLONES. He was Commander of a battle group in the brushmakers' area, a young enthusiast. Twice, during the hardest fighting, when everything seemed lost, when everyone around him was already giving up, he remained on his post alone and fought off the Germans single-handedly, thus saving not only partisan lives, but the lives of hundreds of civilians as well. He did not live to tell the tale.

MEJLACH PERELMAN. As Commander of the Combat Patrols in the Central Ghetto, he led his men himself on several occasions, penetrating to the very Ghetto Walls. During the last patrol he was wounded three times by German rifle fire. A severe stomach wound almost immobilised him, but he did not relinquish his leadership. He covered the patrol's withdrawal to its base. When the base was reached, however, he was unable to enter through the narrow passage and had to remain on the outside. His comrades made him as comfortable as possible in one of the outside rooms and left an armed guard at his side. When the Germans approached at 11am, he gave his arms and ammunition to the guard 'so it may serve further' and ordered him to join the others inside. He remained upstairs alone, and perished. His voice could be heard from amidst the flames for a long time.

DAWID HOCHBERG. He was a battle group commander in the Central Ghetto. Almost a child, his mother wanted to save him so badly that she forbade him to join the ZOB. When the Germans approached a bunker where five battle groups and several hundred civilians were sheltered and their death seemed inevitable, David relinquished his weapons and blocked the narrow passageway with his own body. In this position he was killed by the Germans, but before his wedged-in body could be removed, the entire civilian group as well as the partisans had time to leave the endangered shelter.

TOBCIA DAWIDOWICZ. A liaison woman between the Schultz and Toebbens areas during the fighting, she walked that horrible path under fire more than a dozen times. When she led her group for the last time, to the sewer entrance, she sprained an ankle and could no longer walk unaided. Her friends helped her along, but when, the last in line, she was about to enter the sewer trap-door, she said: 'I shall not come along, I do not want to make the difficult passage still more difficult for you...' And she remained in the Ghetto, alone, where she perished.

On 10 May, 1943, the first period of our bloody history, the history of the Warsaw Jews, came to an end. The site where the buildings of the Ghetto had once stood became a ragged heap of rubble reaching three stories high.

Those who were killed in action had done their duty to the end, to the last drop of blood that soaked into the pavements of the Warsaw Ghetto.

We, who did not perish, leave it up to you to keep the memory of them alive—forever.

Appendices

Reports of the Ghetto uprising
sent out of Poland
by Bund organisations

Appendix one:

Battle of the Warsaw Ghetto

Report from the Jewish workers'
underground movement, 22 June 1943

What follows is an excerpt from a report by the Jewish Labour Underground of Poland, which reached the American representatives of the General Jewish Workers Union of Poland—the Bund—through underground channels via London. It is dated 22 June 1943.

...A characteristic trait of this new extermination campaign waged by the Germans against the Jews is *armed resistance* on the part of the Jews. During the previous wave of extermination such acts of armed resistance were seldom dared. Once in a while we would receive word about such desperate deeds from one small town or another. Now, the entire situation has changed radically. The leading role is being played by the Ghetto of Warsaw.

The first clashes on the streets of the Warsaw Ghetto occurred from 19 until 23 January 1943. That was the beginning of the battle between the armed German Police, SS men and the Jewish Armed Resistance Organisation, which made its first appearance at that time. The January clashes were an embarrassing surprise for the Germans, and were very promising for the future—a prelude of events to come.

Unfortunately lack of space prevents us from describing the historic events that occurred in the Warsaw Ghetto after the January clashes with the precision and esteem that even the smallest detail deserves. This must and shall be done at some future date.

The fight between the Jews and the Germans in April and

May, 1943, that which has been termed the 'Battle of Ghettograd' (Ghettograd—reminiscent of the stubbornness of Stalingrad), eclipses everything that has ever occurred in the annals of the Jews or any other people. The methods and means of the fighting, forced on the belligerents by the special circumstances in the Ghetto, varied in accordance with the various phases of the Battle.

The heart-breaking picture of the Ghetto in flames —shrouded in smoke, the noise of machine guns, cannons, field artillery, mine explosions, the destruction of blocks of buildings, the hell that was unleashed on our people—will forever remain in our memory. No man of letters, no painter will ever be able to recreate the greatness of the events we witnessed, nor the emotions that overwhelmed us during those tragic and historic days.

The Battle that began on 19 April lasted about a month. However, even at the end of May, there was still some resistance.

The backbone of the entire battle was the Jewish Armed Resistance Organisation, which led the people into the fight. This organisation is the armed body of the Coordinating Committee, which comprises an equal number of representatives of the Bund and the Jewish National Committee. Neither the Revisionists [a Zionist group], nor the Agudah [religious Jews] belonged to the Jewish Armed Resistance Organisation. The Revisionists organised a small 'Organisation for vengeance' of their own, which ceased to exist after the second day of the Battle. Workers and youth formed the majority in the Jewish Armed Resistance Organisation. The youngest was Lusiek, thirteen years of age, a member of a Bund youth group, Skif. The oldest member of the organisation was forty. All the members of the resistance organisation were idealists, adherents of various political trends. Their fraternity in battle (Bundists, Chalucym, Shomrim, and others) was exemplary.[1] The general attitude of the inhabitants of the Ghetto towards the idea of resisting the Nazis changed radically from what it was a year ago. It would be wrong and unjust to presume that the heroic spirit and determination of the defenders of the Ghetto was but a result of despair. Many a fighter had ample opportunity to rescue himself by leaving the Ghetto. However, the fighters were full of a noble sense of duty, a soldier's duty, of a powerful desire to carry on the fight for honour, for human dignity. They were anxious to take revenge on Fascism, on the enemy of their people, on the enemy of mankind. The precautions of the Germans bordered on cowardice. The prolonged heroic resistance of the Ghetto banished the legend of the invincibility of the German Army, showed the Polish nation its vast possibilities in resisting the Nazis and strengthened its self-reliance. The 'Jewish-German War' lent strength to the splendid spirit of resistance against the Germans, with which the Polish Underground had already been marked.

Being perfectly aware of this situation, the Germans gave vent to their rage and fury by turning the entire Ghetto into one mass of ruins. On the fifth day of the Battle, the Jewish Armed Resistance Organisation published a manifesto addressed to the Polish Underground, and to the inhabitants of our capital, conveying greetings from the Jewish Underground fighters. Various sectors of the Polish Underground Labour Movement immediately responded with messages of solidarity and admiration. On the whole, the attitude of the Polish Underground towards the Battle of the Warsaw Ghetto was marked with respect for the fighters and with esteem for their daring. However, this attitude varied in accordance with the different viewpoints on the Jewish problem of the various parts of the Polish Underground. The capital city of Poland, as well as the entire country, seethed with excitement because of the Battle of the Ghetto. During the Battle, the Coordinating Committee of the Bund and the Jewish National Committee issued daily communiqués on the Battle, which appeared in Polish clandestine publications and were broadcast abroad by the Polish clandestine radio station Swit.

The result of the Battle was: several thousand Jews were killed, burnt alive, suffocated by gas and about twenty-five thousand were deported to the concentration camps of

Trawniki, Poniatow, Majdanek and Lublin. Only the ruins of buildings, destroyed by mines, cannons and fires remain where the Ghetto once stood. The Warsaw Ghetto is now one big cemetery. Somewhere in the catacombs hundreds, and perhaps thousands of those who survived the battle are still living in agony. Only two days ago, for example, a thirteen-year-old boy appeared from this subterranean world with a message dated 10 June, informing us about 'life' in the modern catacombs. The entire bombardment of Warsaw in 1939 caused the destruction of 75,000 homes, while the present Battle of the Warsaw Ghetto ended with the destruction of one hundred and several thousand homes. As for German casualties: more than one thousand were killed or wounded and tremendous material losses were suffered by German war production enterprises that were set on fire and destroyed by the Jewish Armed Resistance Organisation. The casualties suffered by the Resistance Organisation were comparatively small, but many of its best members, including its commander-in-chief (M Ordche—Hashomer), Engineer Klepfisz, Armament Chief, and Berek, both members of the Central Committee of the Bund, fell in the fight.

When various detachments of the Jewish Armed Resistance Organisation that struggled separately in different sections of the Ghetto were compelled to cease fighting, mainly because they had run out of ammunition, they tried to reach the outlets of this Hell. At that time some two hundred members of the organisation were still alive. The first messenger who brought us word about the desperate struggle of the remnants of the organisation was Frydrych. a member of the Bund, who was prominent in our pre- war athletic organisation, *Jutrznia*. A former soldier in the Polish Army, he was a man of unusual bravery and courage. Not long after he accomplished his mission, he, together with a detachment of fighters of the Resistance Organisation, was captured by the enemy outside of the Ghetto and shot. He made his last journey through subterranean channels to reach us well aware of the importance of his task, and accomplished it against tremendous odds and under unusually dramatic circumstances. Those members of the Resistance Organisation who remained alive tried to get out of the Ghetto through underground channels and passages. It was a fantastic undertaking, accompanied by untold difficulties and danger. Several detachments, numbering some seventy people in all, managed to reach the forest under sensational circumstances. Several other detachments were caught by the Nazis, either at the outposts of the Ghetto or already outside of the Ghetto, but they died fighting until their last round of ammunition. The remaining members of the Resistance Organisation, some sixty of them, did not manage to reach the outposts of the Ghetto and probably died in the underground channels, surrounded by the Germans.

The Warsaw Ghetto, as well as the others, has officially ceased to exist. An official statement, proclaiming the death penalty for all Jews, and for anyone found sheltering them, speaks of the 'former Jewish Ghettos'. Now, in the midst of a new wave of extermination, we are receiving urgent demands for weapons from the ghettos. However, we have very few left. That is why the resistance of the Jews is now not what it was in Warsaw. There are places, however, where Jewish resistance to their Nazi oppressors is even more stubborn than before. The example set by the Battle of the Warsaw Ghetto has influenced everyone. Unfortunately, circumstances prevented us from waging similar battles everywhere.

Warsaw, 22 June 1943
C K R Z M P w POLSCE

Appendix two:

Second report from the Jewish workers' underground movement, 15 November 1943

A second report on Jewish resistance to the Nazis was written six months after the first. This was more wide-ranging, and included details of resistance elsewhere in Poland. Again, what follows is excerpts:

4. COORDINATING COMMITTEE

In July, 1942, a committee was established in Warsaw to co-ordinate the efforts of our organisation [the Bund] with those of the Jewish National Committee. The new group's activity in this regard has brought fruitful results (armed insurrections of January and April, 1943). Following complete liquidation of the Warsaw Ghetto, the activity of the Coordinating Committee embraced the entire sphere of material relief for the Warsaw Jews, and for all of Poland. This committee is neither a political body, nor a communal representation of the Jewish populace; it is merely a unit coordinating the activities of both organisations in the field of relief and struggle.

Paragraph two of the committee's statutes states: 'Political matters shall be settled by each party in accordance with its world outlook.' Within the Coordinating Committee, we have been active in aiding the smaller cities and towns, along with the camps in the field of relief and preparation for armed rebellion. We have assisted the Coordinating Committee with substantial sums for relief of Jews and non-Jews alike, who were active in the Relief Council for Jews, and had been arrested in their line of duty.

We have dispatched aid to various camps amounting to hundreds of thousands of *zlotys*. The Coordinating Committee has neither a treasury nor a treasurer of its own; however, all matters are aired, agreed upon, and unanimously decided upon by both parties. In settling a number of committee matters, many of our comrades play an important part in trying and hazardous positions. The committee spokesmen have conferred with the official military representatives of underground Poland on preparation for the armed rebellion in the Warsaw Ghetto.

5. ARMED STRUGGLES.

During the period covered in this report, a number of armed insurrections flared up around many centres. These struggles represent a continuation of the chain of heroic deeds which the Warsaw Ghetto initiated.

a) First of all BIALYSTOK. This is one of the cities which had, before the war, been strongly influenced by the Bund. The Jews of Bialystok put up fierce resistance when the Nazis began to liquidate the Ghetto in mid-August, 1943. The armed rebellion lasted a month, and was conducted with remarkable heroism. In Bialystok the Nazis again brought into play the methods and ammunition which they employed in Warsaw. Nazi losses in the latter city were high. The Bialystok Ghetto, which numbered 30,000—many of them victims of the uprisings—was liquidated. The surviving population was shipped to the Trawniki labour camp.

b) TREBLINKA. This death camp, where the Nazis annihilated hundreds of thousands of Jews, met total destruction at the hands of the Jews who had been enslaved there, in the early part of August, 1943. The revolting Jews slaughtered the entire 30-men Nazi guard unit that had patrolled the camp. They seized the ammunition, set fire to the buildings, destroyed all electrical communication lines, and blazed a path to the neighbouring woods. Two hundred Jews fled.

c) Jewish rebellions on a smaller scale occurred in TARNOV, BENDIN, CZENSTOCHOW, BORISLAW.

d) Heroism characterising the Treblinka revolt also marked the SOBIBOR rebellion. In Sobibor, too, hundreds of Jews were murdered. The revolt, which occurred in October, 1943, culminated in the successful escape of a large number of Jews from that camp.

e) In conclusion, I should like to cite the resistance which the Lodz Ghetto Jews have displayed on a number of occasions, and which, while they were unarmed, was nevertheless intense and heroic. In February, 1943, a general strike swept the Lodz Ghetto because of the launching of mass-executions by the Nazis. The strike was successful; the executions were halted.

I should also like to mention the Jewish camps of PONIATOW and TRAWNIKI, where armed rebellions, with the aid of the Co-ordination Committee and Jewish armed resistance organisation, which dispatched funds, ammunition and instructions to them, took place. Our comrades who, in the camps, comprise the greatest majority, are very actively preparing for the tasks ahead.

PARTISAN GROUPS.

As I have already previously noted, in connection with ghetto liquidation, certain groups periodically flee to the woods and sometimes affiliate with partisan groups whom they meet along the way. We have devoted a great deal of attention to the matter of how to organise, link, and unite these units. We have also discussed the problem at a number of meetings with spokesmen of the Polish underground military organisation.

MANIFESTO TO THE POLES:

The following is the text of a manifesto addressed to the Poles, which was issued by the Jewish Armed Resistance Organisation during the first days of the Battle of the Warsaw Ghetto in April, 1943:

'Poles, citizens, soldiers of Freedom! Through the din of German cannons, destroying the homes of our mothers, wives and children; through the noise of their machine-guns, seized by us in the fight against the cowardly German police and SS men; through the smoke of the Ghetto, that was set on fire, and the blood of its mercilessly killed defenders, we, the slaves of the Ghetto, convey heartfelt greetings to you. We are well aware that you have been witnessing breathlessly, with broken hearts, with tears of compassion, with horror and enthusiasm, the war that we have been waging against the brutal occupant these past few days.

'Every doorstep in the Ghetto has become a stronghold and shall remain a fortress until the end! All of us will probably perish in the fight, but we shall never surrender! We, as well as you, are burning with the desire to punish the enemy for all his crimes, with a desire for vengeance. It is a fight for our freedom, as well as yours; for our human dignity and national honour, as well as yours! We shall avenge the gory deeds of Oswiecim, Treblinka, Belzec and Majdanek!

'Long live the fraternity of blood and weapons in a fighting Poland!

'Long live freedom!

'Death to the hangmen and the killer!

'We must continue our mutual struggle against the occupant until the very end!

'*Jewish Armed Resistance Organisation*'

It is but fitting that on the anniversary of the Battle of the Warsaw Ghetto we should supplement our previous reports with a detailed description of the activities of the Jewish Armed Resistance Organisation and of our own part in the armed resistance against the Nazis.

From the outset, the uprising was led by the Jewish Armed Resistance Organisation, which comprises Jewish Zionist elements as well as representatives of our party.

Before relating the story of the Jewish Armed Resistance Organisation, we would like to outline our own situation and the circumstances which led to the establishment of this body.

You were informed through the report sent by Janczyn [one of the leaders of the Jewish Underground Labour Movement killed in action], that the first rumours about the mass extermination of Jews in gas-chambers (Chelmno) reached the Jewish community of Warsaw in February, 1941. Our youth organisation Zukunft immediately called a meeting to discuss ways and means of defence should the mass slaughter of Jews spread throughout the General Government [the part of Poland occupied by Germany but not as yet incorporated in the Reich]. The meeting unanimously decided to wage armed resistance. However, at that time, the layman did not believe the appalling truth of the unheard-of atrocities of the Germans.

The first conference of Jewish political parties to discuss the possibility of waging armed resistance did not take place until January, 1942. This conference did not succeed in creating a Joint Armed Resistance Organisation. The participants did not know each other well enough at that time and most of them were afraid lest information about the creation of such an organisation would reach the Germans and give them an excuse to further persecutions.

After this conference, our own Central Committee, at that time located behind the Ghetto walls, commenced organising a self-defence organisation consisting exclusively of members of our party. Its activities were strictly confidential. From its inception, our self-defence organisation was in close contact with the Polish Socialist Organisation (RPPS). Three persons were appointed to lead our self-defence organisation [names cannot be divulged]. Some of the officers of our self-defence detachments were: Abram Fajner, Frydrych Zalmen, Kostrynski Szmul, Lejbel Szpichlerz and Marek. The members of our self-defence organisation received their military schooling from instructors of the PS [Polish Socialists]. The most active members of the self-defence organisation were former members of our Skif and Zukunft [youth organisations of the Jewish Labour Movement before the outbreak of the war]. The names of the following persons, who are known to you, will give you an idea of the elements who joined our self-defence organisation: Jurek Blones, Janek Bilak, Gabrys Fryszdorf, Jankiel Gruszka, Natan Liebeskiend, David Peltz, Welwel Rosowski, Szperling, Pola Lifszyc (intelligence), Cywia Waks (intelligence), and others.

The most difficult task for us, who were shut behind the Ghetto walls and denied all contact with the world, was to provide our self-defence organisation with weapons. At that time no one even dreamt of hand-grenades. To buy and hoard a sufficient number of pistols was difficult enough. However, time passed quickly and soon we were confronted with a new situation. The deportation of the Jews from that part of Poland incorporated into Germany was almost completed. Only the Jews of Lodz were left there and the Ghetto of Lodz had become a closed concentration camp.

In the spring of 1942 the Germans had already commenced with the deportation of the Jews from the smaller towns in the General Government. Even a large Jewish community in one of the more important cities of Poland had already suffered a deportation, but the Jews of Warsaw still did not believe that the same horrible fate was in store for them too. They stubbornly insisted that the capital of Poland would be spared.

On 18 April 1942, the first flash of armed resistance occurred in the Ghetto. Our self-defence organisation paid dearly for its boldness. Our comrades Szklar (printer), Naftula Leruch, Mojsze Goldberg, Taube, Libder and Szajn [all well-known members of the Jewish Labour Movement, Bund] died as soldiers for freedom. After these events there wasn't a quiet night in the Ghetto any longer. Nevertheless, the layman still did not believe that a '22 July' would come [22 July was the fatal day on which the wholesale deportation of 500,000 Warsaw Jews towards death began]. Our **Weker** [the clandestine newspaper of the Jewish Underground Labour Movement] kept urging the Jewish population to resist. However, the Jewish police, together with the Jewish hirelings of the Gestapo as well as some of the elements close to the Kahal [Board of the Jewish Community] went out of their way to prevent an uprising of the Jews. After 22 July, 1942, while the deportation of the Jews of Warsaw was being brutally carried out, a second conference of all Jewish political parties took place. Not being able to convince them, even at that time, to wage armed resistance, we issued an appeal of our own to the Jews of Warsaw revealing the truth about the dreadful fate that was being prepared for them by the Nazis and calling for armed resistance. Lacking sufficient weapons, we called upon the Jews to resist with their bare arms. The following is a quotation from a leaflet issued at that time:

'Don't let them snatch you. Defend yourselves even if only with bare hands.'

[A page or two of the report, following this quotation, was apparently lost on its way from Poland, via London, to us. Despite all their efforts, our delegation in London was unable to find the lost pages.]

The Jews still did not believe. Only when, on the sixth day of the deportation, Zalmen Frydrych (Zygmunt) returned after having followed a transport of Warsaw's Jews who were being sent to the death camp of Treblinka, and publicised his story; only when other Jewish underground groups commenced writing letters to house committees relating the same terrible truth did a part of the Jewish youth of Warsaw finally begin to believe, although the majority of the Jewish population, particularly the older generation, even at that time, stubbornly refused to face realities, to recognise the truth. Even at that time, if anyone mentioned armed resistance, the reply of those Jews was: 'It will only provoke disaster for us all. They will deport every one of us. Don't you know the beastly manner in which the Germans apply collective responsibility?'

After the first week of the deportation, the various identification papers, issued by all kinds of shops, factories and institutions, were invalidated. The only untouchables left were the members of the Jewish Police. Throughout the deportation, our self-defence groups were on the alert, ready to resist and to die. We expected the momentary arrival of a large transport of the long wished-for weapons. The 'five-member groups' of our Skif and Zukunft were mobilised, as well as all available party members. Everyone waited impatiently for the promised weapons, but they did not come... We were finally compelled to demobilise our resistance groups.

It was of great import to us to provide the members of our defence organisation with means to escape deportation. We had not given up hope for an armed resistance, and they were our best fighters. We established close connections with the Polish Socialists who helped us substantially in our task to hide our future fighters. Some of them were rescued four or five times from the *Umszlag Platz* [the deportation place where Germans gathered the doomed Jews]. We want to mention comrades Marjan Merenholc, Olek Kasman, Jerzy Hertz and Mietek Domb, who especially distinguished themselves by rescuing our members from deportation by the Nazis. They willingly risked their lives whenever we needed them.

After the so-called cauldrons [we don't just know what the 'cauldrons' refer to], when such a tremendous number of our comrades perished, the *Umszlag Platz* was still in operation, although the deportations were temporarily stopped. We utilised this time to rebuild our own Resistance Organisation. We simultaneously again tried to contact the representatives of the ZKN [Jewish National Committee] in an effort to establish a mutual resistance organisation.

At the end of October, 1942, a Co-ordinating Committee was appointed consisting of one representative of the ZKN and one of the Bund [Jewish Labour Movement of Poland]. Our representative was A Blum [died a soldier's death]. We also appointed our comrade X as our representative in the ZOB [Jewish Armed Resistance Organisation]. At that time, the membership of our own resistance organisation became quite numerous. The trouble was that we had so few weapons.

The officer in charge of our resistance detachment, which operated on the territory of the brush factories, was Grylak and, of the one who operated on the territory of Tebens [a German military production firm in Warsaw] was Szloma Paff. We had resistance detachments assigned to all other territories, but they had no firearms. The small number of such weapons, which we finally received in December, 1942, from the Underground Polish forces, couldn't satisfy even a fraction of our needs.

Two attempts to assassinate the chief of the Jewish Police, Jacob Leikin, and the liaison officer with the Germans, Israel First, lent popularity to the ZOB. The Jews already knew the truth about Treblinka and consequently no longer trusted the German denials. The Jewish masses finally understood that their death verdict had been signed and that their only hope to rescue themselves was armed resistance against the murderer, and passive resistance of those among them who were unarmed. Some people in the Ghetto dug hiding spots for themselves in order to escape deportation by the Germans, which was bound to start again sooner or later. The ZOB simultaneously began liquidating hirelings and servants of the Jewish Police and the Gestapo. Members of our party, outside of the ZOB, were of great help in the work of cleansing the Ghetto of the above-named elements. However, we were still not entirely prepared to meet the second deportation of the remnants of the Warsaw Ghetto by the Germans.

We had already received weapons at that time. The trouble was that they were not yet distributed among the members of the ZOB. The weapons were still stored in our clandestine Central Warehouse. That is why only the resistance groups located in the vicinity of this Warehouse were able to wage armed resistance. During the days of those first flashes of armed resistance, Abraham Fajner, our faithful comrade, died in action.

Although the armed resistance waged at that time, in January, 1943, did not embrace the entire ghetto, because of the mentioned circumstances, and was confined to a rather small section of it, the significance of this first attempt can hardly be overestimated. During this first armed battle against the Germans, the legend of an invincible German, holding the life and death of hundreds of thousands of Jews in his hands, vanished. Our fighters, concentrated in five spots, mainly waged guerrilla warfare against the Gremans. Nevertheless, several more important battles took place.

The biggest battle broke out on the corner of Zamenhofa and Stawki Streets. The Germans, totally surprised by the armed resistance of the Jews, stopped the deportation after two days. This unexpected success greatly increased the prestige and the role of the ZOB. The authority of the ZOB [Jewish Armed Resistance Organisation], after the January battles, grew steadily from day to day.

At that time, the ZOB governed the entire life of the Ghetto. For example, at the request of the ZOB, the Jewish Community Council contributed one million *zlotys* towards the sole purpose of buying weapons. This amount was paid in cash within a period of three days.

Being unable to perform their planned deportation of the Warsaw Jews by means of lies and false promises, the Germans finally resolved to deport the remaining Warsaw Jews forcibly. On 19 April, 1943, at two o'clock in the morning, the Germans surrounded the Ghetto walls with many guards (every 25 metres), consisting of German, Ukrainian and Latvian Fascist soldiers. Carefully, in singles, in twos and in threes, the German soldiers entered the Ghetto. But this time we were prepared. At four o'clock, before dawn, all our resistance groups were mobilised and at their assigned positions. They were prepared to meet the hated enemy. The number of armed resistance detachments were: eight in the centre of the Ghetto, five in the territory of the brush factories, and seven in the vicinity of the big Schultz and Tebens factories.

At six o'clock in the morning, on 19 April, 1943, 2000 armed SS men, along with tanks and cannons, three trucks loaded with ammunition and an ambulance entered the Central Ghetto. The entire German deportation staff followed the SS army. Among the members of this deportation staff were the following officers of the Gestapo and SS: Michelsen, Handke, Hoffle, Mireczko, Barteczko, Brand and Mende. There were no Jews to be seen anywhere. All of them were hidden in subterranean, previously prepared trenches and holes of all sorts. Only the members of the ZOB remained on the surface and were on the alert. Our fighters were concentrated to defend three strategic points, barring entry into the main streets of the Ghetto.

The first armed battle took place on Nalewki Street where two resistance units, behind barricades, defended the street. The battle there lasted six hours and brought about the first defeat of the Germans. The Germans retreated, leaving behind many of their soldiers who had been killed. Simultaneously the main battle raged on the corner of Zamenhofa and Mila Streets. Our fighters, after building barricades to shut off the four corners of those streets, daringly attacked the main German detachment, which had entered the Ghetto. After the first salvos from machine-guns and hand-grenades were successfully aimed at the compact ranks of SS men, the entire street was deserted. The green uniforms of the Germans were no longer to be seen anywhere. They took shelter in nearby stores and gates and exchanged some shots with the defenders of the Ghetto. After a cessation of fifteen minutes, tanks appeared. They came quite close to the spot where our fighters were gathered. After a while, incendiary bombs, calmly and carefully aimed, set the first tank on fire. The flames spread with unexpected swiftness and soon there was an explosion. The tank was lost. The other tanks immediately left, together with the panic-stricken Germans. Their retreat was covered with renewed gunfire and grenades. The German casualties numbered 200, killed and wounded. We lost only one soldier. After two hours, the Germans brought cannons, which were placed outside of the Ghetto, and successfully bombed the spot of their previous defeat. They took our defence strongholds, and freed the entrance into the Ghetto.

Suddenly, from the windows of the other side, Zamenhofa 29, grenades were thrown. This was the second attack against the Germans, which was being carried out on the same place by one of our resistance groups, that had deliberately not participated in the previous battle, lest its whereabouts should be discovered. Fifty Germans were killed. Our group escaped without any casualties. At five in the afternoon, there were no longer any Germans in the Ghetto. They left the Ghetto in order to gather somewhere on a deserted territory nearby. Our temporary success had been a result of the suddenness and quickness of our resistance, performed from well-disguised spots.

The second day of the Battle of the Warsaw Ghetto, 20 April, 1943, began with a large concentration of SS detachments, along with artillery, on the territory between the Ghetto and the Aryan districts (Plac Krasinskich). However, they had not as yet dared enter the populated Ghetto streets. At about three o'clock in the afternoon, a detachment of 300 SS men arrived near the gate to the district of the brush factories. They stopped for a little while, but this brief pause was sufficient for our fighters to cut an electric wire, which caused a mine explosion under the very feet of the SS men. The Germans ran away, leaving 80 to 100 killed and wounded. Only after two hours did they come back.

After the previous costly experience, they were now more careful and alert. Thirty SS men entered the gate to this district. Our fighters, hidden in selected spots, waited for them. Grenades and incendiary bombs met the Germans. Only two of the 30 SS men escaped. Those who were not hit by grenades burned alive. But now the Germans brought their artillery into the battle. The district was shelled from all four sides. In the meantime, two high officers from the SS came into this district. They appealed to our fighters to put down their arms and proposed a fifteen-minute truce. Our fighters replied with more gunfire. From the other side of the district, somewhere near Franciszkanska Street, a second detachment of SS men tried to reach our fighters. Met by several well-aimed shots, this detachment gave up also and turned back. Once more the entire district was clean of Germans. That was the second complete victory for our fighters.

On the same day, 20 April 1943, in the vicinity of the large Schultz and Tebens factories, the Germans called upon the Jews to volunteer for forced labour camps, but their appeal was in vain. All the inhabitants of this district, just as the inhabitants of the Central Ghetto, were hidden in subterranean caves. The management of Schultz and Tebens kept prolonging the time limit in which the Jews could volunteer, but met with no success. When the management of Schultz and Tebens declared that it was compelled to apply the same methods as in the Central Ghetto, our resistance groups that were concentrated in this district attacked a detachment of SS men with bombs and grenades somewhere on the Aryan side of the city, as well as German detachments who were on their way to the Central Ghetto through Nowolipie and Smocza Streets. The

Germans suffered 40 killed and many more wounded.

Executing a personal order issued by the Chief of the German Police in Lublin-Globocnik, who came to Warsaw to lead the Battle of the Ghetto, the Germans started setting the entire Ghetto on fire on the second day of the uprising. At first, they set fire to the buildings and street blocks where they had suffered from our resistance—Nalewki 33, 35, 37, Mila 28, 29, Zamenhofa 28 and, finally, the entire district where the brush factories were located. This was the first large conflagration. Thousands upon thousands of people perished in the flames. People were burned alive in their hide-outs as well as in their homes and on the rooftops. A jump from the third or fourth floor usually put an end to the lives of burning Jews. Those who succeeded in escaping the fire were shot on the street by the Germans. Many corpses were found in a sitting position. Those were people who had been killed while sleeping. A very common spectacle were corpses of women with children in their arms.

In retaliation for the Ghetto fire, our fighters set fire to all the German *Verterfassum* stores [war materials collections], as well as to their large shops, which were worth millions of *zlotys*.

Conflagrations did not stop our resistance. The Germans hunted for our hide-outs. It was not difficult for the Germans to find them, because the terrible heat drove the Jews out of their hiding places, particularly at night, when they gathered in their backyards. They usually left traces leading to their hide-outs. The Germans successfully employed the use of bloodhounds and sounding devices to find the hidden Jews. At that time our fighters had already dropped their offensive tactics and were on the defensive. Their task was to rescue, as far as possible, those who were still alive in their hide-outs. This task required a regrouping of our armed forces.

Our detachments were now assigned to defend many of the still-existing hide-outs. On the sixth day of the Battle of the Warsaw Ghetto, 24 April, 1944, defensive battles occurred in the territory of Schultz and Tebens. Our fighters barricaded themselves in some buildings and on rooftops in an effort to prevent the Germans from reaching the hidden Jews. For many days our fighters defended the Jewish population that was in hiding. The bloodiest of these fights took place at Nowolipki 41, Leszno 78, 76, 74, Nowolipie 67, 69. All in all our offensive and defensive battles lasted ten days.

Our meagre ammunition was already disappearing. The bits that were left were used exclusively for self-defence and guard duty.

According to our accounts the Germans suffered about 1200 casualties killed and wounded. Sporadic fights, waged by our fighters against the Nazis, took place long after the Battle of the Warsaw Ghetto was over. They occurred primarily at night. The Germans burned the Ghetto systematically. After two weeks the entire Ghetto, as well as previously decimated districts, ceased to exist. Lack of water and food rendered impossible the life of those who still fought. The Germans then commenced burning down buildings. They hoped to destroy, together with the houses, the remaining dug-outs and nests of our fighters and to break their will to fight. The Germans used gas bombs...

During this final period of the last struggle against the Germans who invaded and seized our dug-outs one after another, or suffocated the fighters by means of gas bombs, the majority of the ghetto defenders died. A large number of the officers in charge of the Jewish Armed Resistance Organisation gathered in a special dug-out and committed suicide in order to escape from the clutches of the Germans. Only a small fraction of them was able to escape through the city's sewers and reach the Aryan districts. The four resistance groups that still remained in the Ghetto waged guerrilla warfare against the Germans for a month. All of the members of these four groups perished. Thus, the Battle of the Warsaw Ghetto lasted almost seven weeks.

Our party was a member of the Jewish Armed Resistance Organisation for more than six months (from October 1942 until May 1943). We joined hands with all Jewish Zionist underground organisations. Our comrades lived and worked with the others just as members of a close family. A mutual aim united us. During this entire period of over half a year, there were no quarrels or struggles, which are common among adherents of different ideologies. All overworked themselves in organising the mutual defence of our dignity. All fought equally in this historic life and death struggle. There was no difference between the members of our party and the others in regard to sacrificing themselves or performing their soldier's duty until the very last... However, we are reporting here primarily about our own members.

At the beginning of the battle, in January 1943, we possessed four well-organised resistance detachments of our own. The officers in charge of them were: Jurek Blones, Welwel Rozowski, Lejwik Granzalz and Dawid Hochberg. Our comrade X led the entire resistance of the brush factories' territory. Our comrades, who had been active before the January 1943 battles, were on the Co-ordinating Committee and the General Staff of the mutual Jewish Armed Resistance Organisation. The following of our comrades were members of the Auxiliary Committee of the ZOB, located in the Aryan districts of Warsaw: Frydrych, S Fund, Celemenski, Wladka-Peltel-Fajga. Michal Klepfisz led and organised the entire production of hand-grenades and incendiary bombs in the Aryan districts, as well as in the Ghetto.

The majority of all our fighters was killed in action, either in the Battle of the Warsaw Ghetto or immediately after reaching the Aryan districts through the sewers. Jurek Blones, who led our resistance group in the district of the brush factories, was one of the most brilliant and gallant fighters. Twice during the battle he rescued his detachment from sure death by alone engaging an entire detachment of attacking Germans. Mejlack Perelman, on his beat around the Ghetto walls, though wounded by three German shells, nevertheless for a long time covered the escape of his comrades. When he could no longer stand on his feet, he turned his gun over to one of his comrades, knowing how precious weapons were. We took him to the backyard, near the dug-out of his group, but he could not walk in. He was too weak. We carried him upstairs and put him in a certain room. When our man who was on duty called on him and wanted to help him, Perelman did not permit him to stay. 'Take the rest of my weapons,' he said. 'I cannot use them any more, but you will need them.' On the following day, the Germans set fire to the building he was in and he was burned alive.

Tobcia Dawidowicz, a liaison officer of our resistance group in the Schultz and Tebens territory, though wounded in the leg, nevertheless successfully led her group towards the sewers in order to help them escape. Not wanting to become a burden to her comrades, she remained in the Ghetto after all her comrades had entered the sewers.

Dawid Hochberg was an officer in charge of a resistance detachment in the Central Ghetto. When the Germans discovered the dug-out of his comrades, he handed his gun over to one of them and barricaded the entrance into the dug-out with his own body. It took the Germans 15 minutes to remove his body from the small entrance. In the meantime, the fighters of his group, along with other Jews that were hidden in the cave, escaped through another exit.

We can relate many other stories such as these about our fighters who struggled and died as heroes. Those comrades who functioned as collaborators with the ZOB during the Battle of the Warsaw Ghetto also died. They were: Luzer Klog, Grylak, Kiersz, Bluma Klog, Renia Pizyc, and many others.

The Jewish Armed Resistance Organisation continues its activities even now, after the Battle of the Warsaw Ghetto, establishing new contacts and maintaining old ones. Our representative is still on the General Staff of this organisation and in the Co-ordinating Committee, which supervises its work.

The representative of our party in the Aryan district branch of the ZOB, who was in contact with military and civil authorities of Underground Poland in conjunction with the entire existence of the Warsaw Ghetto was comrade... In July 1943, the Co-ordinating Committee appointed two of its members for the same purposes, one in behalf of our party, the other in behalf of the ZK [Jewish National Committee].

The ZOB now has several detachments, one of which is

active in Warsaw. The others are located in various country places. Our comrades, who were put at the disposal of the ZOB, are the messengers, who always contact the detachments in the country and provide them with money, clothing, medicaments, letters and weapons. One can guess what a difficult and dangerous job it is to maintain such contacts. The ranks of the armed detachments of the ZOB are today sparser because of the counter-measures applied by the Germans and the activities of certain vicious bands [we don't know what kinds of bands the report refers to]. In general, the task of maintaining our contacts with the country is growing more and more difficult.

Notes

INTRODUCTION

1. In Poland the Bund was the largest Jewish workers' organisation,
    being both a workers' party and a trade union. In the documents
    published here, it is referred to by various names: the Jewish
    Socialist Party, the General Jewish Workers Union of Poland, the
    Jewish Labour Movement of Poland—all are references to the Bund.
    The Polish Bund had its origins in the Jewish Workers Bund of
    Russia, Lithuania and Poland, which developed in the Tsarist
    empire before the Russian revolution of 1917. The Bund was always
    part of the revolutionary socialist movement in Russia, though its
    ideas were more akin to those of the Mensheviks than the
    Bolsheviks. Polish Bund leader Henryk Erlich had been a leader of
    the Menshevik faction in the Petrograd Soviet in 1917.
    Lenin repeatedly engaged the Bund in sharp polemics over its
    demand for national cultural autonomy. For a discussion of this, see
    Tony Cliff, **Lenin: All power to the soviets 1914–1917**
    (Bookmarks: London 1985) chapter 3.
    The Polish Bund, however, was uncompromising on the question of
    the emigration of Polish Jews to Palestine. It repeatedly accused the
    Zionists of collaboration with the anti-semites on this matter.
    Unfortunately most of the documentation concerning this remains
    untranslated in the original Yiddish in the Bund publications of the
    day. However, something of its flavour can be gained from the only,
    and all too brief, English language history of the Polish Bund,
    Bernard Johnpoll's **The Politics of Futility** (Cornell University
    Press: New York 1967):
    'The Polish regime's proposed solution for the "Jewish problem"
    was similar to the Zionists'; namely mass emigration... The Bundists
    were quick to note the similarity... A Bund leader noted that Ben
    Gurion, the leader of the World Labour Zionist Movement, along
    with Greenbaum, leader of the liberal General Zionists, and

Jabotinsky, leader of the extremist Revisionists, agreed with the enemies of the Jews... The Bundists called this treason to the Jews... Bund leader Victor Alter said: "The theory of Greenbaum that Jews are 'excess baggage' in Poland is dangerous nonsense, which must be strongly rejected." ' (Johnpoll, pages 216-7).

2. A typical passage is: 'The most positive force to rise from the ashes of the Holocaust was the "new Jew"... the Jew who would fight to survive... the outstanding example of this new Jewish attitude was the Warsaw Ghetto uprising... though of greater symbolic than practical import... The place where the "new Jew" was most clearly emerging was in Palestine... the first Jewish fighting force in the Holy Land for nearly 1800 years.' (Abba Eban, **Heritage, Civilisation and the Jews** (Channel 4 Books: London 1984) pages 310-2). In general, latter-day Zionists have adopted a double standard towards Jewish resistance to the Nazis. They both defend Zionist leaders who refused to fight the Nazis, and at the same time they have attempted to 'fit' Jewish struggles against the Nazis into the so-called struggle for Palestine.

3. For a discussion about this commemoration, see my article in **International Socialism**, 2:44 (London: Autumn 1989).

4. As the introduction to the American edition of **Shielding the Flame** put it: 'the tremendous response that it elicited from Polish readers showed that not all was as dark as it seemed. A new generation of Poles were not satisfied with what their parents, their state and their church were telling them—or rather not telling them—about the Jewish part in Polish history.'
Edelman's English language translator wrote of his involvement in Solidarity: 'I think he was looking in Solidarity for the same things he'd experienced in the ZOB, the Jewish Fighting Organisation in the Ghetto—the closeness, fraternity, all these fundamental things...'

5. Edelman told me he did not agree with our view of how socialism can be achieved, but had no objection to the Socialist Workers Party publishing **The Ghetto fights** because once published it would be public property. Obviously, he is in no way responsible for my introduction. Concerning socialism, he told me: 'Everyone has his own meaning of the word. If it means in economic terms a state economy then it is a failure. My idea of socialism is no state monopoly. There should be stress on the subjectivity of the human being. You need good material conditions, a high level of culture, much freedom and friendship. And it won't come today or tomorrow. It's a long and winding road...' (Interview with Marek Edelman at his home in the Polish city of Lodz, 21 March 1989).

When I met Edelman he was extremely busy with the 'Round Table' negotiations between Solidarity and the Polish government which led Solidarity to enter the government later in 1989. He led the discussions for Solidarity on relations between Poland's national minorities. He discusses his role in this in a long interview in **Studium Papers**, an American-Polish publication, volume 13, number 2 (April 1989).

6. Trotsky's major writings from this period are to be found in Leon Trotsky, **Fascism, Stalinism and the United Front** (Bookmarks: London 1989).

7. Leon Trotsky, 'The Turn in the Communist International and the German Situation', in Trotsky, **Fascism, Stalinism and the United Front**, page 41.

8. Isaac Deutscher, **The Prophet Armed** (Oxford University Press 1970) page 133.

9. Abram Leon, **The Jewish Question** (Pathfinder Press: New York 1970) page 236.

10. Abram Leon, page 237.

11. Abram Leon, page 238.

12. Leon Trotsky, 'Germany, the Key to the International Situation', quoted in Isaac Deutscher, **The Prophet Outcast** (Oxford University Press 1963) pages 143-4.

13. Leon Uris, **Mila 18** (London 1961) page 85. This famous novel is still often the only book people have read about the Warsaw Ghetto. It reads rather like a soap opera today and has a strong political bias against the Bund. However it certainly captures the ruthlessness of the Nazis and later the amazing courage of the Ghetto fighters.

14. Neal Ascherson, **The Struggles for Poland** (Channel 4 Books: London 1987) pages 96-100.

15. Ascherson, page 94.

16. Zofia Nalkowska, introduction to Marek Edelman, **The Ghetto fights** (American Representation of the General Jewish Workers Union of Poland: New York 1946).

17. Hannah Krall, **Shielding the Flame** (Henry Holt: New York 1986) page 8.

18. Marek Edelman, **The Ghetto fights**, see above page 56.

19. Yisrael Gutman, **The Jews of Warsaw 1939-43** (Harvester Press 1982) page 230.

20. Antony Polonsky (editor) **A Cup of Tears: A Diary of the Warsaw Ghetto by Abraham Lewin** (Blackwell: Oxford 1988) page 288, note 159.

21. Gutman, page 289.

22. Emmanuel Ringelblum, quoted in Reuben Ainsztein, **Jewish Resistance in Nazi-occupied Europe** (Elek Books 1974) page 593. Ringelblum was a left Zionist who organised the secret underground archive of the Ghetto. He slipped successfully in and out of the Ghetto for three years before he was finally caught by the Nazis and murdered. Much of his writing remains untranslated in the original Yiddish in archives in Jerusalem, despite the resources of the Israeli government.
23. Bund leaflet quoted in Edelman, **The Ghetto fights**, appendix 2, see above page 103.
24. Ringelblum, quoted in Ainsztein, page 593.
25. Ainsztein, pages 903-4, note 4.
26. Ainsztein, page 594.
27. Quoted in Ainsztein, page 651.
28. Quoted in Ainsztein, page 671.
29. See for example the books by Ainsztein and Gutman.
30. For a discussion of this, see the book by Ascherson.
31. Edelman, **The Ghetto fights**, see above page 68.
32. Interview with Marek Edelman, 21 March 1989.
33. Manifesto quoted in Edelman, **The Ghetto fights**, appendix 2, see above page 99.

THE GHETTO FIGHTS

1. The German armies had invaded Poland on 1 September, 1939, though Warsaw itself did not surrender until 26 days later.
2. When the occupying German authorities wanted a work party for any reason, they simply rounded people up randomly from the streets. This was often done simply as a means of harassment.
3. 'Aryan' was the term used by the Nazis to distinguish the North European races from others that were considered alien and inferior, in this case the Jews.
4. For more information on the Bund, see above: Introduction note 1.
5. The Skif was the Bund's organisation for schoolchildren, arranging self-education courses, summer camps, excursions and other similar activities.
6. In Greek mythology Cerberus was the three-headed watchdog that guarded the gates of the underworld.
7. The Zukunft—the word itself means 'Future'—was the Bund's youth organisation, whose aim in normal times was to spread socialist ideas among Jewish young people.
8. The Hashomer and Hechalutz were left-wing Zionist youth organisations; in Hebrew *Hashomer* means 'Young Guards' and *Hechalutz* 'Young Pioneers'.

9. This was the left wing of the Polish Socialist Party (PPS).
10. The Jewish resistance organised itself into groups of five people, called 'fives'.
11. These were well-known children's plays.
12. Four forces policed the Ghetto: the *Schutzpolizei* were the Ukrainians; 'gendarmes' were the Germans and the 'navy-blues' the Polish police; the fourth was the Jewish Police.
13. The General Government was that part of Nazi-occupied Poland not yet incorporated into Germany.
14. *Umsiedlungsstab* means 'resettlement unit staff'.
15. The PS and WRN were the left and right factions in the Polish Socialist Party.
16. The Dror was a right-wing Zionist youth movement, the PPR the Polish Communist Party.

APPENDIX ONE

1. The Chalucym and Shomrim were other names for the Hechalutz and Hashomer respectively.

Other publications from Bookmarks

Fascism, Stalinism and the United Front / *Leon Trotsky*
The victory of the Nazis in Germany in 1933 was a defeat for the
working-class movement of undreamt-of magnitude—yet it was
avoidable. Trotsky's analysis of the class forces involved remains
unparallelled. 272 pages. £4.95 / $9.95

Festival of the Oppressed / *Colin Barker*
The trade union Solidarity shook the Eastern bloc to its
foundations in 1980- 81. This book tells the story of its rise and
analyses the weaknesses that lay behind the setback in 1981. 272
pages. £4.25 / $8.50

Racism, resistance and revolution / *Peter Alexander*
Racism is neither natural nor irrational, but a product of the social
system that rules our lives. This book looks at the success and
failure of different attempts to fight racism—and at how it can
ultimately be defeated. 186 pages. £3.95 / $8.50

Israel: The hijack state / *John Rose*
A brief outline of the history of Zionism and the state of Israel,
showing the role that Israel plays in the world system as
'watchdog for the West'. 80 pages. £2.50 / $4.75

Intifada / *Phil Marshall*
Following the mass uprising of Palestinians in Israel's occupied
territories, this book exposes the structure of domination of which
Israel is the keystone: an imperialism whose foundations lie in
Britain 100 years ago and the US today—and which oppresses the
workers of the Arab countries as much as the Palestinians. 256
pages. £5.95 / $11.00

The Quiet Revolutionary
The autobiography of Margaret Dewar

A schoolgirl in Moscow during 1917, forced to flee during the
famine years, then a revolutionary socialist in Germany during
Hitler's rise to power—this is the autobiography of one of the
'ordinary' people who are the real movers of history. 224 pages.
£5.95 / $11.95

The Lost Revolution: Germany 1918-23 / *Chris Harman*

Revolutions that are deafeated are soon forgotten—yet the defeat
of the great working-class upheavals that shook Germany after the
First World War was a key link in the rise to power of both Hitler
and Stalin. 336 pages. £5.95 / $11.00

Russia: From workers' state to state capitalism
/ *Peter Binns, Tony Cliff and Chris Harman*

In 1917 the hopes of millions were placed on the workers'
revolution in Russia—but what went wrong? This book offers hard
answers to tough questions. 112 pages. £2.50 / $4.75

June '36 / *Jacques Danos and Marcel Gibelin*

The election of the French Popular Front government in June 1936
seemed at last to put socialism on the agenda. Workers greeted it
with mass strikes and demonstrations, watched with horror not
just by bankers and employers... but by the Popular Front leaders
themselves. 272 pages. £5.95 / $11.95

All available from good bookshops, or by post from Bookmarks
(add 10 per cent to cover postage—minimum 35p or $1).

BOOKMARKS

265 Seven Sisters Road, London N4 2DE, England.
PO Box 16085, Chicago, IL 60616, USA.
GPO Box 1473N, Melbourne 3001, Australia.